Sustainable Project Management: The GPM Reference Guide

Joel Carboni
William Duncan
Mónica Gonzalez
Peter Milsom
Michael Young

Copyright Information

Printed in the United States of America

2nd Edition 2018

ISBN 978-0-578-19688-6

GPM Global
23491 Haggerty Rd.
Novi MI 48375, USA

www.greenprojectmanagement.org

Contents

List of Tables

List of Figures

Notes

Preface

Our planet is facing greater challenges than ever before including bio-diversity loss, population increases, constrained natural resources, human induced climate change, and social and economic inequality.

Although a growing number of organizations are establishing strategies to combat these issues, implementing a change of this magnitude is not easy as many of today's organizations were founded at a time when *sustainable* meant having a healthy bottom line.

Over the past decade, however, the definition of *sustainable* has evolved and many organizations have had to re-evaluate their business to incorporate practices that are socially responsible and environmentally friendly. It is, therefore, necessary to align the management of projects, to better support the new business landscape, the blue economy. It goes without saying that evolving the project management profession's role has never been more critical.

To achieve sustainability as a planet, we must increase our capacity to be able to go beyond sustainable development and remediate the problems that humans have caused to the planet while driving forward. With the challenges humanity is facing, whether they be geopolitical conflicts, climate change, extreme poverty, resource scarcity, slavery, or inequality in all its forms, the profession of project management must play a more signifigant role. This second edition of our reference guide is a major redesign and focuses on *how* to manage projects sustainably.

This book is aimed at anyone involved in projects. It provides a starting point for understanding both the principles of sustainable project management and the PRiSM methodology.

The concepts we present are ever-evolving, and we are excited to bring this reference guide to benefit the project management profession.

Dr. Joel B. Carboni
Founder, GPM

Notes

How to Use This book

The aim of this book is to provide awareness of and practical information on how to manage projects sustainably. If you are involved in projects in any capacity, this book is for you. Our goal is to provide practical information and step-by-step guidance that can be kept at your desk as a reference as you do project work.

We have divided this book into four parts and fourteen chapters:

- **Part One** — provides the context and underlying motivation for sustainability and sustainable project management.
- **Part Two** — outlines the PRiSM Methodology and the approach to sustainable project management.
- **Part Three** — provides the underpinning concepts for sustainable project management.
- **Part Four** — provides an overview of the many international standards that support sustainable project management.

This book is best used as a reference, rather than reading it from cover to cover. This book is also used as a resource to support a number of GPM programs.

Notes

PART ONE: Sustainability

Notes

1. The Sustainability Imperative

1.1. Why Sustainability?

Humanity has been misled by economic models that devalue our natural resources. By economic models that endanger our ability to survive as a species. By economic models that consider profit as the only indicator of business success.

In the place of these models, business leaders around the world are increasingly responding to demands by investors, employees, and consumers to use models that reward low-carbon and environmentally sustainable products and services.

The driving force behind these demands is concern for the long-term viability of life-as-we-know-it in the face of human-induced climate change. Research has made it clear that the sixth mass-extinction — and the first since the Ordovician-Silurian Extinction roughly 439 million years ago where 86% of life on Earth disappeared — is upon us. According to proceedings from the National Academy of Sciences (PNAS, 2015) in the United States, nearly half of the 177 mammal species surveyed have lost more than 80% of their distribution between 1900 and 2015. The ecological, social, and economic impacts associated with biodiversity loss of this magnitude are unknown.

Sustainability is also needed to solve other global challenges such as extreme poverty, inequality, and lack of access to quality education. Innovation and opportunity must be placed at the forefront setting the tone for an agile, progressive, and productive global economy.

By early August of each year (soon to be late July), humans will have consumed what the planet can regenerate. Between January and July, more carbon is emitted than the forests and oceans can absorb for the entire year. We are overfishing, overharvesting, and overconsuming potable water. In all, we consume the natural resources of 1.7 earths a year.

Earth overshoot day, the day in which we have reached our consumption limit, has been moving closer to January each year. It was first calculated in 1986 as falling in November. In 1993, it moved to October, and in 2017 it was August 2nd. Some countries exceed their consumption limit much sooner. The U.K., for example, reaches their consumption limit by early May. The only country to not exceed its limits is Honduras.

One of the reasons for overconsumption is global population increases. According to the UN Population Fund, there are more than 7 billion people in the world which is twice the amount there was in 1970 and four times the amount in 1910. In terms of net gain, we are adding 200,000 people to the planet each day, and according to projections, we are headed to over 9 billion which is unsustainable.

Overconsumption has impacted our oceans by increasing acidification over 30% since the beginning of the industrial revolution according to the U.S. National Oceanic and Atmospheric Agency. The increased acidification levels have caused a bleaching of the Great Barrier Reef in both 2016 and 2017, the first time it has occurred in back to back years. It takes ten years for the fastest corals to recover, and back to back bleaching events offers no opportunity for recovery (Kerry et all, 2017).

1.2. The Evolution of Sustainability Models

In 1994, John Elkington created a well-known model when he coined the term *Triple Bottom Line* (3BL) in his book *Cannibals with Forks*. His argument was that companies should be preparing three different (and quite separate) bottom lines for cost accounting:

- **Profit** — the first bottom line is the traditional measure of financial performance — how responsible has the company been in terms of assuring its competitive prosperity.
- **People** — the second bottom line is the measure of a company's social account — how socially responsible has the organization been in terms of its impact on the quality of life of the individuals it affects.
- **Planet** — the third bottom line is the measure of the company's environmental account — how environmentally responsible has it been in terms of its impact on natural ecosystems.

The Triple Bottom Line aims to measure the financial, social, and environmental performance of a business over a period of time. The TBL comes up short, however, as the three items are difficult to add up or compare. For example, in the infamous 2010 Deepwater Horizon (BP) Gulf of Mexico oil spill, the massive impact on BP's profits was clear, but it was nearly impossible to quantify the people and planet accounts.

In recent years, a *purpose* line has been added (Dodgson, 2010) to fill this void. Purpose also includes adaptive innovation — i.e., adaptive learning and change, trial and error risk taking and discovery — in all aspects of people, profit, and planet.

Clear purpose simplifies decisions about what to innovate and helps define criteria and metrics to observe and measure what is being innovate taking into account the environmental, social and economic impacts.

There are generally four ways that purpose in organizations is measured:

- **Customers** — creating a measure of success based on the positive value that is created for the end user/customer.
- **Employees** — creating a measure of success based on employee well-being and productivity, driven by the creation of meaningful opportunities for them. Paying livable wages, providing quality healthcare, and competence development are a few examples.
- **Suppliers**— creating a measure of success based on sustainable sourcing, transparency, and serving as an ethical influencer throughout their supply chain.
- **Market** — creating and measuring success based on market changes that are linked to the purpose based innovations an organization has demonstrated within its sphere of influence.

Note that *purpose-driven* shouldn't be confused with *goal-oriented* in that if the organization lacks purpose it may have an inherent assumption that their goals are value-creating when they may not be. Rather, it means weaving purpose-driven environmental and social considerations into the fabric of how the organization operates as well as what its goods and services are.

Most representations of the Triple and Quadruple Bottom Lines depict three or four overlapping circles of equal size. We did not as the concepts do more than overlap: society is wholly contained within the natural environment and the economy is a subset of society. The nested dependency model shown below depicts the Quadruple Bottom Line. Prosperity is placed as a dependency on purpose.

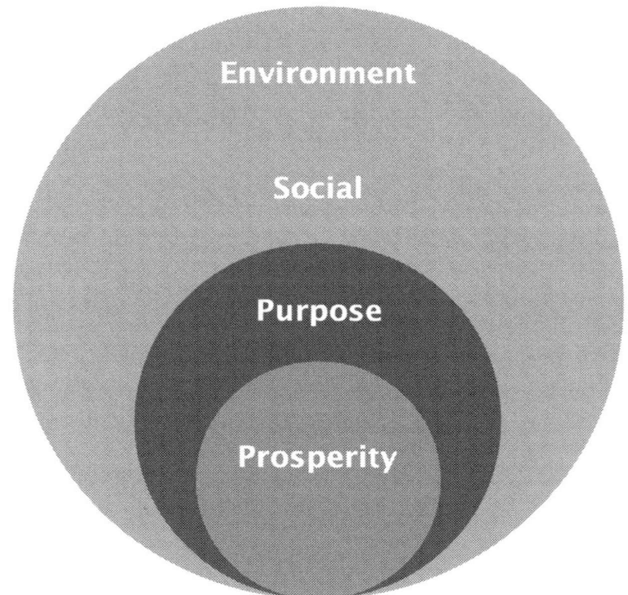

Figure 1-1: Nested Dependency Model

The *Blue Economy* concept shown in Figure 1-2 below aims to address these shortcomings by redefining the concept of waste through a self-sufficient approach. It also aims to prevent the use of materials which can only be used once and discarded, transitioning from the common linear structure that has dominated since the industrial revolution, to a systems-based model that challenges the consumption of resources based on their necessity for production.

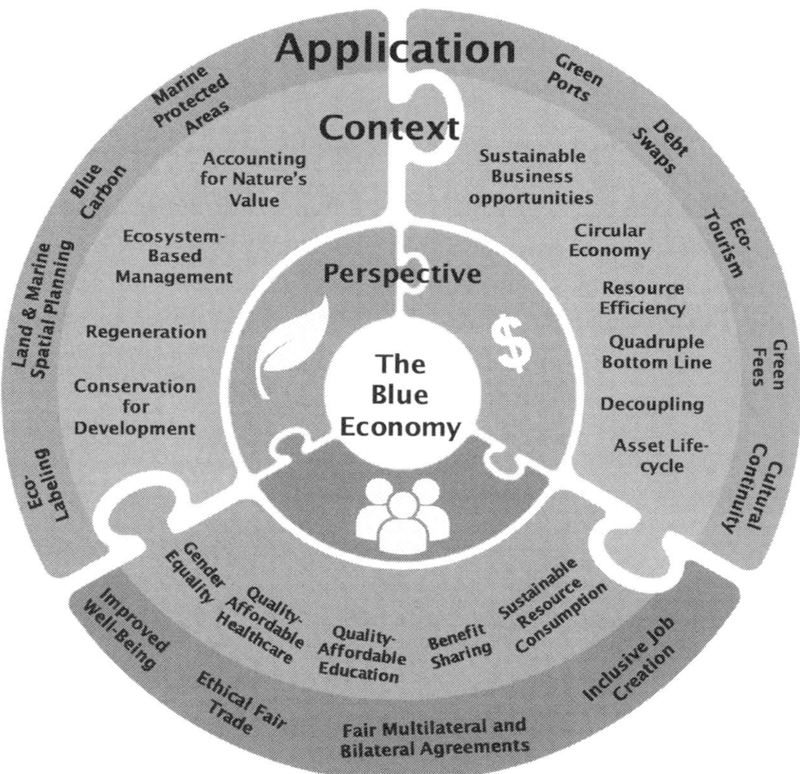

Figure 1-2: The Blue Economy Model

With this shift, waste becomes nonexistent and by-products become the source for new products thus regenerating the environment and establishing healthy and vibrant economies.

The Blue Economy model emphasizes local economic development and the entrepreneurial spirit inspired by nature and ecosystem designs where waste does not exist. By learning from nature, we can regenerate our planet, solve global crises, and create a world where future generations can thrive.

The Blue Economy model moves away from misleading economic health indicators such as Gross Domestic Product (GDP, which is no more than the culmination of market transactions), to measures that focus on the actual health of the economy and society. For example, GDP does not take into account the level of debt a country has, the cost to service that debt, or the level of corruption in a country. Increases in GDP are often accompanied by negative impacts on the people and planet bottom lines.

.Several new models are being utilized to transform how countries view social and economic progress. The Gross Happiness Index (GHI) was developed in Bhutan and measures the collective happiness in a nation. The Genuine Progress Indicator (GPI) has grown in adoption in Canada and the United States and takes into account the costs of adverse effects related to economic activity such as crime, carbon outputs, and biodiversity loss.

1.3. Why Organizations Adopt Sustainable Practices

As illustrated in Figure 1-3 below, there are several reasons why organizations adopt sustainable practices:

- **Crisis Management** — only responding to sustainability issues such as an oil spill or human rights abuse issue.
- **Regulatory Compliance** — adopting a sustainability policy in order to remain compliant with laws, regulations, and guidelines so as to remain in business.
- **Resource Optimization** — developing sustainability strategies to optimize resources in order to reduce costs or increase efficiency.
- **Purpose Driven** — mobilizing staff and other resources sustainably in order to create value and generate sustainable growth.

For example, an organization may begin to adopt better sustainability practices after a crisis such as an environmental disaster that they caused. Another organization may adopt sustainable practices out of a need to comply with relevant regulations. In both cases, the drivers for their choices would be risk mitigation and brand protection.

More mature organizations will still want to mitigate their risks and protect their brand, but they will also see sustainability as a source of future benefits. They will usually start off with a focus on resource optimization with an expectation of realizing greater productivity.

As an organization's maturity continues to grow, it will seek to use sustainability as a way to differentiate itself from its competitors or to help penetrate new markets. It will enjoy the benefits of increased productivity while still mitigating risks and protecting its brand.

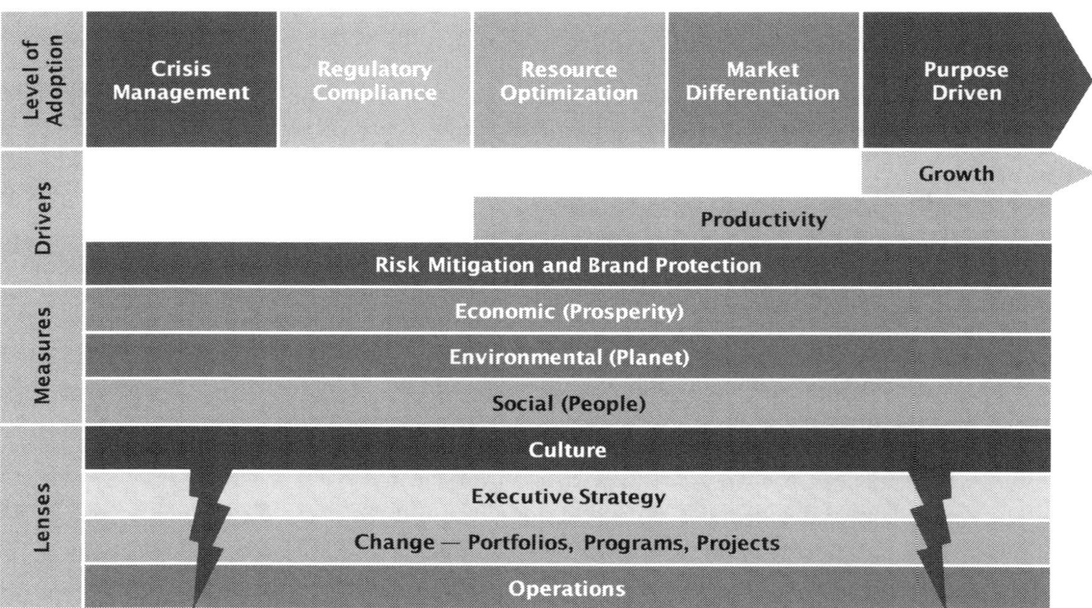

Figure 1-3: Levels, Drivers, and Measures of Sustainability Adoption

The most mature organizations are *purpose driven*: sustainability is core to their existence and their growth. An example of a company that is purpose driven is Method Soap. They are one of the fastest-growing private businesses in the United States. They set out to develop a high quality, unique product that would be socially and environmentally responsible. Method collaborated with beach clean-up organizations in Hawaii and a recycled plastics leader, Envision Plastics, to collect tons of ocean plastics to use for their bottles. In the bottles, they use environmentally friendly ingredients rather than sodium hypochlorite so they do not pollute the water tables.

Figure 1-3 also outlines the relationship between the levels of adoption and their measures. These measures are in line with the aforementioned sustainability models using the three perspectives of environmental, economic, and social. The lenses, shown at the bottom of the figure, represent the aspects of the organization where sustainability policies need to be adopted and put into practice in order to be effective in achieving the benefits tied to each driver.

1.4. The Sustainable Development Goals

In 2011, Colombia proposed the adoption of seventeen Sustainable Development Goals (SDGs). The United Nations, together with business leaders, governments, the science community, and others came together in support of the SDGs as the best way to address the sustainability challenges our world faces. This support was affirmed in a resolution from the 2012 RIO+20 Conference which is commonly known as *The Future We Want* and a subsequent 2012 report titled *Realizing the Future We Want.*

Shown below, the SDGs build on the successes of the Millennium Development Goals (MDGs), which expired in January of 2015.

Figure 1-4: United Nations Sustainable Development Goals (SDGs)

While the SDGs include new areas such as climate change, economic inequality, innovation, sustainable consumption, peace, and justice, the goals are interconnected so that success on one goal contributes to the success of another. These goals are the single greatest project that humanity has undertaken as a collective.

GPM, an active voice in the United Nations Global Compact, was an actor for the advancement of the goals before their ratification at numerous leadership summits and working sessions. GPM has committed through its standards, tools, and programs to influence projects both locally and globally on how they can contribute to the achievement of these goals. There is a vast amount of information about the SDGs on the web and in the public domain. Organizations and individuals who influence trades and professions should support the goals and contextualize them for their industry as GPM has.

The goals and targets will stimulate action over the next fifteen years in areas of critical importance for humanity and the planet (UN, 2017):

- **People** — to end poverty and hunger, in all their forms and dimensions, and to ensure that all human beings can fulfill their potential in dignity and equality and in a healthy environment.
- **Planet** — to protect the planet from degradation, including through sustainable consumption and production, sustainably managing its natural resources and taking urgent action on climate change, so that the planet can support the needs of the present and future generations.
- **Prosperity** — to ensure that all human beings can enjoy prosperous and fulfilling lives and that economic, social, and technological progress occurs in harmony with nature.
- **Peace** — to foster peaceful, just, and inclusive societies which are free from fear and violence. There can be no sustainable development without peace and no peace without sustainable development.
- **Partnership** — to mobilize the means required to implement this agenda through a revitalized Global Partnership for Sustainable Development, based on a spirit of strengthened global solidarity, focused in particular on the needs of the poorest and most vulnerable, and with the participation of all countries, all stakeholders, and all people.

The interlinkages and integrated nature of the Sustainable Development Goals are of crucial importance in ensuring that they are achieved. And if they are achieved, the lives of all will be profoundly improved, and the world will be transformed for the better.

For more information, visit: https://sustainabledevelopment.un.org/sdgs.

1.5. United Nations Global Compact

The *United Nations Global Compact* (UNGC) is a CEO-driven initiative where thousands of companies around the world work together to advance the Ten Principles of sustainable business within their sphere of influence and to make public their commitment to their stakeholders.

The principles provide guidance for sustainable business behavior and are the underlying principles for the SDGs.

Category	Principle	Businesses should ...
Human Rights	1	Support and respect the protection of internationally proclaimed human rights
	2	Make sure that they are not complicit in human rights abuses
Labor Standards	3	Uphold the freedom of association and the effective recognition of the right to collective bargaining
	4	Uphold the elimination of all forms of forced and compulsory labor
	5	Uphold the effective abolition of child labor
	6	Uphold the elimination of discrimination in respect of employment and occupation
Environment	7	Support a precautionary approach to environmental challenges
	8	Undertake initiatives to promote greater environmental responsibility
	9	Encourage the development and diffusion of environmentally friendly technologies
Anti-Corruption	10	Work against corruption in all its forms, including extortion and bribery

Figure 1-5: UNGC Principles

1.6. Sustainability as an Influencer

An organization's commitment to sustainability has become a critical part of measuring its overall performance, and its ability to thrive in the global market.

Sustainability focused organizations around the world are thriving and delivering attractive returns to shareholders as evidenced by the growth of Sustainability Index Funds.

An organization's commitment to sustainability has a direct influence on its:

- Competitive advantage in realizing a favorable or superior business position in the market
- Brand reputation or the level of trust or confidence its brand has among consumers
- Ability to attract and retain workers or members, customers, clients, or users
- Employee morale, commitment, and productivity
- Evaluation by investors, donors, sponsors, and the financial community
- Relationship with other companies, governments, media, and suppliers
- Peers, customers, and the community in which it operates

1.7. Summary

In this chapter, we have examined the Sustainability Imperative and in particular we have identified the key drivers behind why a sustainable future is critical to survival as a human race. The chapter introduced a number of different sustainability models and highlighted how these models have continued to evolve over time as a result of research, critical thinking, and adoption. Sustainability is not just a focal point for environmentalists, but is now a core part of a modern organization. Business and government around the world are now identifying many drivers and as such sustainability makes good business sense, is profitable and can result in product innovation.

The chapter also examines the United Nations Sustainable Development Goals (SDGs) and highlights how they can contribute to a better society and a cleaner environment for future generations. By working with other organizations and targeting specific SDGs, individuals and organizations alike can make a positive contribution. In this book, the focus will be on the application of the SDGs to projects and project management.

The chapter wraps up with an examination of the UN Global Compact and the ten UNGC Principles. These principles are embedded in the PRiSM methodology detailed in Part Two.

2. Sustainability and Projects

Sustainability requires change, and change is almost always delivered through projects. This chapter covers the vital relationship between sustainability and projects.

2.1. Sustainable Projects

GPM defines a project as "an investment that requires a set of coordinated activities performed over a finite period of time in order to accomplish a unique result in support of a desired outcome." Section 4.1.1 contains a detailed discussion of the components of this definition.

For a project to be sustainable, the requirements and constraints must include mitigation of negative environmental, social, and economic impacts and attainment of the benefits outlined in the business case.

A sustainable project will also adhere to GPM's six principles for sustainable projects:

- Commitment and accountability
- Ethics and decision making
- Integrated and transparent
- Principles and values based
- Social and ecological equity
- Economic prosperity

These principles are discussed in detail in Section 3.4.

2.2. Sustainable Project Management

As the project management profession matures, it is changing its view of what project success is. The profession is now moving beyond its traditional focus on time, cost, and scope to placing the emphasis on delivering the objectives in the business case while maintaining an asset lifecycle focus.

The next step in the evolutionary process is to adopt a sustainability ethos where projects do not come at the expense of the planet and its limited resources. Project management must make greater efforts to address each project's social and environmental impacts so that the world we live in and that we are borrowing from future generations can regenerate and be sustained.

In order to take this step, project management must move to a wider and well-rounded view of the project's impact and value as illustrated below.

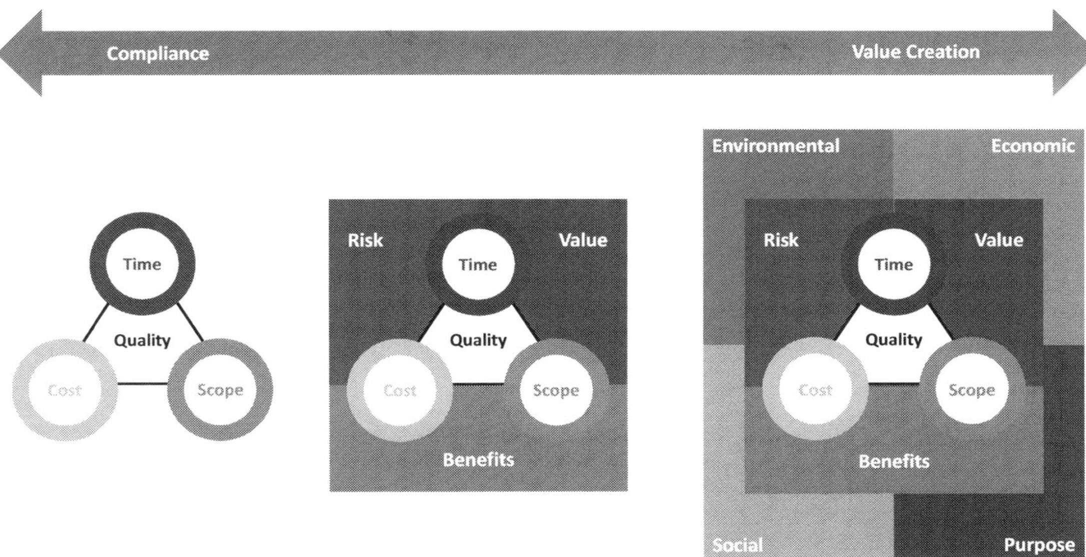

Figure 2-1: The Evolution of Project Management Focus

2.3. The GPM P5™ Standard for Sustainability in Project Management

P5 stands for People, Planet, Prosperity, Process, and Products.

The P5 standard is a tool that supports the alignment of portfolios, programs, and projects with an organizational strategy for sustainability and focuses on the impacts of project processes and deliverables on the environment, society, the corporate bottom line, and the local economy. The elements of P5 describe the actions to be taken by a project manager to deliver a sustainable project in a sustainable way.

P5 is not a methodology for how to create a sustainable project environment; however, it provides the principles and foundation for the PRiSM approach described in Part Two.

The P5 standard represents a structure as it defines something. Since it was first introduced in 2010, it has evolved from a decision matrix to a full ontology that contextualizes sustainability concepts for the project management profession.

P5 is both a periodic table of elements for sustainability measures that should be considered in every project, and a link between projects and the SDGs. It provides guidance on how to integrate sustainability with project management. This book does not include details on P5, but the standard can be downloaded from https://www.greenprojectmanagement.org/p5.

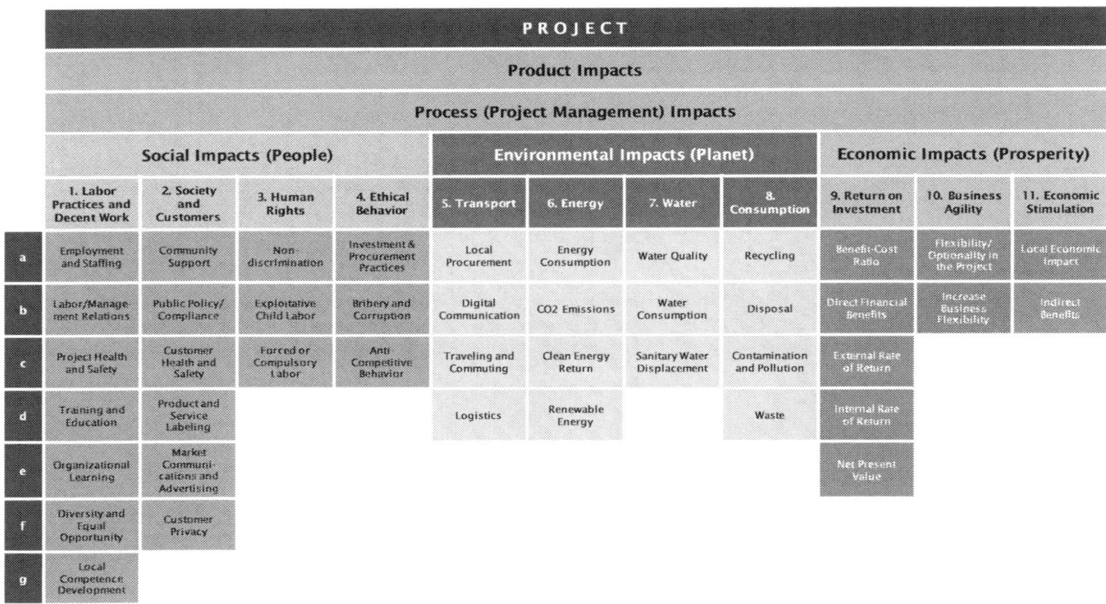

Figure 2-2: P5 Ontology

2.4. Sustainable Project Managers

A *sustainable project manager* is an individual who manages a project by employing a collection of diverse but integrated competencies to deliver on the objectives detailed in the business case. This is done by using and tailoring the appropriate methods, tools, and techniques for leading the project team, engaging stakeholders, and progressing the project while still safeguarding society, the environment, and human rights.

Sustainable project managers contribute to organizational goals while navigating complex cultures and dynamics to create benefits that support short- and long-term business strategies while simultaneously addressing our planetary constraints.

As such, sustainable project managers have an important role to play as advocates, advisors, and architects of a better world.

The following table outlines the characteristics of a sustainable project manager.

Sustainable Project Manager Characteristics
Benefits Focused — is aware of stakeholder needs and expectations, considers long-term implications of decisions
Inclusive Leader — understands what motivates team members and other stakeholders, uses a collaborative approach that builds an environment of trust, values individuals, is open to new ideas
Change Agent — challenges business-as-usual mindset, embraces change, seizes opportunities, develops new ideas, acts positively, is opportunistic, interacts well with others
Ethical — has high moral integrity, uses ethical approaches, establishes trust-based relationships, upholds principles and values, empowers others
Systematic — thinks holistically, identifies relationships and interactions, frames problems and opportunities in patterns over time, focuses on causality as an ongoing process, focuses on context

Sustainable Project Manager Characteristics
Intentional — supports sustainability as an integral, deliberate aspect of project success
Ambitious — continuously develops own competence, takes challenges head on, shows confidence in decision making, conveys self-confidence
Collaborative — supports partnerships with stakeholder groups
Accountable — is transparent, manages risk, seeks out meaningful engagement with stakeholders, is accountable for adverse impacts

Table 2-1: Characteristics of a Sustainable Project Manager

2.5. Summary

This chapter highlights the changing nature of project management and the shift away from the traditional, linear thinking of the past. No longer is it good enough to deliver projects on time, on budget, and to specification. Stakeholders are now demanding a greater emphasis on the benefits to be realized from their investments in projects.

To provide guidance about sustainable project management, GPM has developed the P5 Standard for Sustainability in Project Management and has also developed the PRiSM methodology which will be explained in more detail in Part Two of this book.

3. Ethics, Principles, and Values

True wisdom comes to each of us when we realize how little we understand about life, ourselves, and the world around us. (Socrates)

As discussed in Chapters 1 and 2, business has historically been focused on profit. Even the public and not-for-profit sectors have tended to focus on delivering an excess of revenues over expenses. But today, we have new, broader economic models that are driving organizational leaders to respect human rights, to care for the climate, and to reduce poverty and hunger. This behavior is guided by a new understanding of ethics, principles, and values.

3.1. Core Concepts

Ethics, principles, and values are fundamental to sustainability because they provide guidance about what behaviors and decisions are acceptable:

- **Ethics** — provide guidance for what behaviors are acceptable. Ethics are typically defined by an external agency such as a professional association.
- **Principles** — represent fundamental truths or propositions that serve as the foundation for a system of belief or for a chain of reasoning. Principles are universal, proven in practice, and empowering. Principles are also usually defined externally.
- **Values** — are what individuals consider to be most important in their lives, such as compromise, prudence, courage, hard work, competition, efficiency, thrift, freedom, material success, or patriotism. Values are derived from specific personal beliefs and are influenced by an individual's experiences.

Figure 3-1 below shows the relationship between ethics, principles, and values.

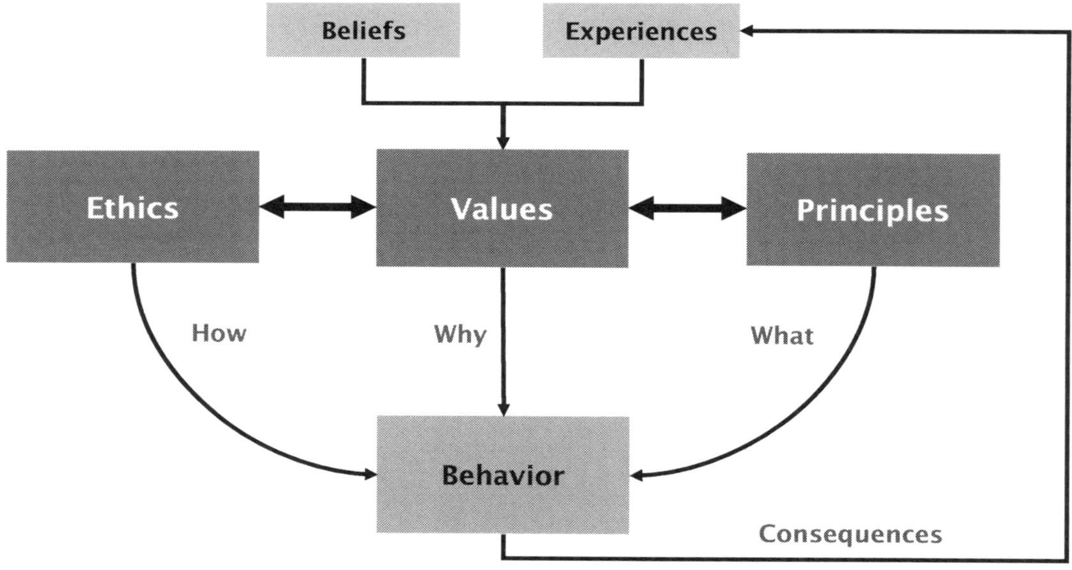

Figure 3-1: Relationship between Ethics, Principles, and Values

3.2. Ensuring an Ethical Supply Chain

A *supply chain* is the system of organizations, people, activities, information, and resources involved in moving a product or service from supplier to customer. A supply chain may include the transformation of natural resources, raw materials, used or recycled materials, and other components into a finished product that is delivered to an end customer. Supply chains are not limited to manufacturing: service providers such as consulting firms also have supply chains.

Ensuring an ethical supply chain is challenging because the customer seldom has direct control over the suppliers. Nonetheless, an ethical supply chain is fundamental to sustainability since it is where much of the social and environmental impacts occur.

Anti-corruption compliance programs should emphasize the importance of fostering an organizational culture that effectively prevents and resists corruption. The aim of these programs should go beyond risk mitigation to helping organizations internalize ethical values by promoting positive behavioral change and creating a values-driven approach to governance.

Organizations are increasingly expected to "know and show" compliance with ethical standards throughout their operations, products, and services.

3.2.1. Benefits of an Ethical Supply Chain

The benefits of ensuring that your organization's supply chain is ethical include:

- Improved product quality
- Reduced fraud and related costs
- Enhanced reputation for honest business
- Internal resilience to meet and manage inevitable crises
- A more sustainable platform for future growth

3.2.2. Costs of a Corrupt Supply Chain

Corruption, broadly defined, may be the single greatest obstacle to economic and social development around the world. Corruption distorts markets, stifles economic growth, debases democracy, and contributes to conflict and instability by undermining the rule of law. The UN estimates that the annual cost of corruption is more than 5% of global GDP (US $2.6 trillion) with nearly 40% of that amount (US $1 trillion) paid in bribes.

Corruption risks in the supply chain include procurement fraud perpetrated by suppliers, often in league with the customer's own employees, and suppliers who engage in corrupt practices with government agencies. The direct costs of this corruption are often dwarfed by the indirect costs related to management time and resources dealing with the issues, such as legal liability and irreparable damage to a company's reputation. Business misconduct is often publicized within hours or even minutes of discovery.

Corrupt practices also have the potential to cause devastating harm to communities and societies via both harmful product quality and deadly safety and environmental disasters.

3.2.3. Human Rights Violations and the Supply Chain

Human rights violations should be considered a special case of corruption in that both pose similar risks to organizations, including the danger of reputational and financial exposure.

Organizations should avoid causing or contributing to adverse human rights impacts and should commit to addressing adverse impacts that do occur. Organizations must seek to prevent or mitigate adverse human rights impacts directly linked to their operations, products, or services by their business relationships even if they have not contributed to those impacts.

Organizations should be able to identify, prevent, mitigate, and account for how they address their impacts on human rights. They should also have in place a process to remediate any adverse impacts they cause or to which they contribute.

Corruption often causes human rights violations. For instance, in India, forced child labor has been linked to failed law enforcement due to corruption. Also in India, in April 2013, Rana Plaza, a commercial building in Dhaka collapsed, killing more than a thousand people and severely injuring at least twice as many. The tragedy is widely attributed to bribes paid to avoid factory approvals and building inspections.

3.2.4. Fighting Corruption in the Supply Chain

According to the *Corruption Perceptions Index Report* (Transparency International, 2016), over two-thirds of the 176 countries and territories in that year's index fall below the midpoint of the scale of 0 (highly corrupt) to 100 (very clean). The global average score was a paltry 43 which indicates endemic corruption in a country's public sector.

Corruption in the supply chain represents a major obstacle to reaching all the SDGs as it hampers economic growth and increases poverty, thus depriving the most marginalized groups of equitable access to vital services such as healthcare, education, water, and sanitation. Nor is corruption only an issue for low-income states: rich countries are affected by cross-border corruption, foreign bribery, tax evasion, and related illicit financial flows.

> *"In too many countries, people are deprived of their most basic needs and go to bed hungry every night because of corruption, while the powerful and corrupt enjoy lavish lifestyles with impunity." (José Ugaz, Chair, Transparency International)*

Good Practice	Description
Risk Assessment	The overall process of assessing the likelihood of fraud and corruption in the supply chain is complex, and not all customer-supplier relationships present the same level of risk.
Cooperation and Education	Moving toward comprehension and capacity building, suppliers should come to understand why preventing corruption and doing business with integrity is in their interest. Customers should look for continuous improvement from suppliers. At the same time, customers must be ready to terminate a relationship where necessary.
Collective Action	Efficiencies can be achieved if customers are willing to accept training or auditing conducted by other customers, and if there is a standard code of conduct to which all customers agree.

Good Practice	Description
Synergy	Supply chain integrity should be monitored through all aspects of a company's supply chain relationship. Companies need to see supply chain management as a unified process with a common set of policies and practices that include corruption prevention as well as the more traditional elements of cost control, quality monitoring, and logistics management.

Table 3-1: Good Practice for Fighting Corruption in the Supply Chain

The following table presents useful questions to consider when evaluating the risk of corruption in your organization's supply chain.

<table>
<tr><th colspan="2">Questions to Ask About the Impact of Supplier Corruption</th></tr>
<tr><td colspan="2">▪ What would happen to your supply chain if a supplier engaged in corruption?
▪ What are the risks to your reputation if such a disruption occurred?
▪ What are the risks to your operations if such a disruption occurred?
▪ What are your potential remedies if you discover a corrupt supplier?
▪ How would you control the damage from a corrupt supplier?
▪ Are there alternative sources of supply? What are they?
▪ Could you be liable because of a supplier's corrupt activities?</td></tr>
<tr><th colspan="2">Questions to ask …</th></tr>
<tr><th>About Your Business</th><th>About Your Suppliers</th></tr>
<tr><td>▪ What internal controls are in place to prevent, detect, and respond to internal fraud?
▪ What internal controls are in place to prevent, detect, and respond to supplier fraud?
▪ What internal controls are in place to prevent, detect, and respond to procurement fraud?
▪ What internal controls are in place to monitor spending limits and ensure documentation review?
▪ What processes are in place for vetting suppliers for potential conflicts of interest?
▪ What processes are in place to monitor suppliers?
▪ What processes are in place for supplier audits and inspections?
▪ Does the overall anti-corruption program meet applicable standards?</td><td>▪ What is the supplier's reputation for integrity and ethical conduct?
▪ Where is the supplier located? What are the corruption risks in those locations?
▪ What is the importance of the contract to the supplier's business? What is the likelihood of kickbacks? What is the likelihood of other kinds of procurement fraud?
▪ What are the possible points of contact with government corruption?
▪ How was the supplier identified? Are there any personal connections?
▪ What controls does the supplier have in place to prevent corruption?
▪ Is the supplier being engaged as an agent to deal with the local government (e.g., to obtain permits or to deal with customs)?
▪ What is the supplier's relationship to their government? Are there personal or business connections?</td></tr>
</table>

Table 3-2: Questions to Ask to Help Prevent Supply-Chain Corruption

To learn more about what prudent customers and suppliers should do, consult the *Practical Guidance on Preventing and Responding to Corruption in the Supply Chain* (UNGC, 2016).

3.3. Ethics and Sustainability

As noted above, *ethics* provide guidance for acceptable business behavior. There are good business reasons for a strong commitment to ethics:

- Ethical companies have been shown to be more profitable.
- Ethical choices result in lower stress for managers and other employees.
- Ethical behavior strengthens leadership by building trust and confidence.

In contrast, unethical behavior may result in negative publicity, declining sales, and even legal action. For this reason, it is necessary to be able to identify and understand the ethical issues that arise, and to develop the knowledge and skills needed to address these issues. Ethical issues are an inevitable element of business decision making and are deeply intertwined with managerial practice and economic activity generally.

3.3.1. Policies and Standards

To help employees determine what conduct is acceptable, organizations should have policies and standards describing what the organization expects of all of its employees, from entry level workers to the highest levels of management. These policies and standards should address:

- **Employee relations.** Employees expect businesses to provide a safe workplace, pay them adequately for their work, and tell them what is happening in their company. They want employers to listen to their grievances and treat them fairly. A major social responsibility for business is providing equal opportunities for all employees regardless of their sex, age, race, religion, or nationality.
- **Consumer relations.** Customers expect businesses to provide them with satisfying, safe products and to respect their rights as consumers. Defective or dangerous products erode public confidence in the ability of business to serve society. They may also result in expensive litigation that ultimately increases the cost of products for all consumers. The right to be informed gives consumers the freedom to review complete information about a product before they buy.
- **Environmental issues.** Environmental responsibility has become a leading issue in the last decade as both business and the public acknowledge the damage done to the environment in the past. Today's consumers are increasingly demanding that businesses take a greater responsibility for their actions and their impact on the environment. Many businesses are trying to respond. For example, automakers are developing vehicles that run on alternative fuels such as electricity, solar power, natural gas, and methanol.
- **Community relations.** A final, yet very significant, issue for businesses is their responsibility to the general welfare of the communities and societies in which they operate. Businesses should make their communities better places for everyone to live and work.

3.3.2. Ethical Issues

> *An ethical issue is an identifiable problem, situation, or opportunity requiring a person or organization to choose from among several actions that must be evaluated as right or wrong. (Ferrell, 2017)*

Ethical issues often arise as a result of:

- **Conflicts of interest** when an employee must choose whether to advance their own personal interests or those of others. To avoid conflicts of interest, employees must be able to separate their personal financial interests from their business dealings.
- **Fairness and honesty** are at the heart of business ethics and relate to the general values of decision makers. At a minimum, businesspersons are expected to follow all applicable laws and regulations. But beyond obeying the law, they are expected not to harm customers, employees, clients, or competitors knowingly through deception, misrepresentation, coercion, or discrimination.
- **Communication** is another area in which ethical concerns may arise. False or misleading advertising, as well as deceptive selling tactics, will anger consumers and can lead to the failure of a business. Truthfulness about product safety and quality are also important to consumers. Accurate product labelling is fundamental to ethical and sustainable behavior.
- **Business relationships** with customers, suppliers, and others may also create ethical issues. Ethical behavior within a business involves keeping company secrets, meeting obligations and responsibilities, and avoiding undue pressure that may force others to act unethically. Managers are responsible for creating a work environment that helps the company achieve its objectives and fulfill its responsibilities. However, the methods that managers use to implement these responsibilities should not compromise consumer, supplier, or employee rights.

Ethical issues are also influenced by the culture in which a business operates. In North America, for example, it would be inappropriate to bring a gift to a prospective client — the gift could be viewed as a bribe. In Japan, however, it is considered impolite ***not*** to bring a gift. Experience with the culture in which an organization operates is critical to understanding what will be considered ethical or unethical.

To support sustainability, the entire project team should understand the differences between the values, morals, and ethics of the other stakeholders. Transgressing another person's beliefs will affect how they judge you.

3.4. Principles and Sustainability

Recognizing the increased interest of project managers worldwide to be agents of change who are aligned to the high standards needed to address today's sustainability challenges, GPM recommends that all project managers (as well as all program and portfolio managers) should adhere to GPM's *Six Principles of Project Management Sustainability.*

Commitment and Accountability	Recognize the essential rights of all to healthy, clean, and safe environments, equal opportunity, fair remuneration, ethical procurement, and adherence to the rule of law.
Ethics and Decision Making	Support organizational ethics and decision making with respect for universal principles through identification, mitigation, and the prevention of adverse short- and long-term impacts on society and the environment.
Integrated and Transparent	Foster the interdependence of economic development, social integrity, and environmental protection in all aspects of governance, practice, and reporting.
Principles and Values Based	Conserve and enhance our natural resource base by improving the ways in which we develop and use technologies and resources.
Social and Ecological Equity	Assess human vulnerability in ecologically sensitive areas and centers of population through demographic dynamics.
Economic Prosperity	Adhere to fiscal strategies, objectives, and targets that balance the needs of stakeholders, including immediate needs and those of future generations.

Table 3-3: GPM's Six Principles of Project Management Sustainability

3.4.1. Commitment and Accountability

Sustainable project managers should demonstrate their commitment to the essential rights of all to healthy, clean, and safe environments, equal opportunity, fair remuneration, ethical procurement, and adherence to the rule of law.

Accountability comes from transparency which is discussed below in Section 3.4.3.

3.4.2. Ethics and Decision Making

Sustainable projects managers should demonstrate their support for ethics and ethical decision making. They must work to identify, mitigate, and prevent adverse short- and long-term impacts on society and the environment.

One of the best ways to do so is by ensuring that their project's business case addresses:

- Relevant principles and values
- Compliance with their organization's sustainability governance
- Regulatory compliance
- Organizational sustainability objectives
- Project sustainability objectives
- Economic, environmental, and social performance indicators
- Social responsibility requirements

3.4.3. Integrated and Transparent

Sustainable project managers should contribute to fostering the integration of economic development, social integrity, and environmental protection in all aspects of governance, practice, and reporting. By adopting a leadership role in promoting the organization´s contributions to sustainability, project managers will contribute to benefits from improved supply chains, better coordination among local and regional agencies, and more effective public-private partnerships.

To help ensure transparency, project managers should assume that any available information can be shared unless there is a clear reason not to (e.g., proprietary information). For example, many companies now share salary information to minimize the potential for gender discrimination.

Transparency can also help decision makers outside of the project as they tackle social, environmental, and economic challenges such as:

- Protection of human rights
- Policies and action plans to address climate change
- Reduction of waste and ecosystem contamination
- Reduction of wealth inequality
- Management of social conflict and migration
- Re-education of workers for new competences and skills
- Reinforcement of anti-corruption policies

3.4.4. Principles and Values Based

Sustainable project managers should demonstrate that they conserve and enhance the natural resource base by improving the ways in which their employers develop and use technologies and resources. For example, they can support sustainable economic models such as the blue economy by reducing resource consumption and waste, by minimizing ecosystem contamination, by respecting human rights, and by creating value for society as a whole.

3.4.5. Social and Ecological Equity

Sustainable project managers should assess human vulnerability in ecologically sensitive areas and centers of population through demographic dynamics.

The growth of world population and production combined with unsustainable consumption patterns places increasingly severe stress on the life-supporting capacities of our planet. These interrelated processes affect the use of land, water, air, energy, and other resources. There is a need to increase awareness of this issue among decision makers at all levels in order to develop strategies to mitigate both the adverse impact on the environment of human activities and the adverse impact of environmental change on human populations. In that sense, project managers can play an important role by:

- Improving understanding of the relationships among demographic dynamics, technology, cultural behavior, natural resources, and life support systems.
- Assessing human vulnerability in ecologically sensitive areas and centers of population to determine the priorities for action at all levels.

- Identifying priority areas for action and developing strategies and programs to mitigate the adverse impact of environmental change on human populations.
- Promoting awareness of the need to optimize the sustainable use of resources through efficient resource management, taking into account the development needs of the populations of developing countries.
- Promoting awareness of the need to improve the status of women by providing access to education, primary and reproductive health care programs, and economic independence.

3.4.6. *Economic Prosperity*

Sustainable project managers should demonstrate adherence to strategies that balance the immediate needs of stakeholders with those of future generations. This means being aware of how their projects affect environmental concerns, vulnerable population groups (e.g., rural landless workers, ethnic minorities, refugees, migrants, displaced people, women heads of household), the alleviation of poverty, secure livelihoods, good health, quality of life, and improvement of the status of women.

3.5. Values and Sustainability

Sustainability starts with a shared value system and a principled approach to doing business. This means operating in ways that meet fundamental responsibilities in the areas of human rights, labor, environmental protection, and anti-corruption.

This shared value system is often called *organizational culture.* It is the unique way that an organization defines itself in terms of its worldviews, principles, traditions, customs, rituals, stories, practices, and unwritten rules that distinguish it from other organizations.

Shared values are the heart of every organization — the glue that binds it together — creating an internal cohesion that supports achievement of its business goals. An organization whose values are aligned with its employees and other stakeholders will be able to fully harness their energy and creativity. It will have a culture which is collaborative, resilient, productive, and fully motivated to achieve those goals.

The United Nations Global Compact (UNGC), the world's largest corporate sustainability initiative, calls for companies to align their cultures with universal principles and to take actions to advance the SDGs. The UNGC Ten Principles (see Section 1.5) enjoy universal consensus and are derived from:

- The Universal Declaration of Human Rights (1948)
- The International Labour Organization's Declaration on Fundamental Principles and Rights at Work (1998)
- The Rio Declaration on Environment and Development (1992)
- The United Nations Convention Against Corruption (2003)

The number of organizations who adhere to the UNGC Ten Principles and put stock in sustainability is increasing even though doing so may require many aspects of the organizational culture to evolve or change. Adjustments may be needed to the way it conducts business, as well as the way it treats its employees, its customers, and the environment of which it is a part.

The organizational culture affects productivity, customer service, marketing and advertising practices, human rights policies, and the capacity for innovation. Increasingly, it also includes its environmental and social responsibility practices.

3.6. Summary

This chapter focuses on ethics, principles, and values and the critical role they play in the modern organization. In the past, private sector companies would undertake a range of less than acceptable practices in the name of boosting shareholder returns and of growing their share price. In the modern era of social media, these actions are being called out by lobbyists and concerned citizens and the organization's social license to operate is being called into question. No long is it acceptable to make millions in profits by ripping off the poorest people in society or creating environmental disasters.

Ethics in the organization's supply chain is now of critical importance. Society expects organizations, their suppliers, and their entire supply chain to be free from human rights abuses, slavery, child exploitation, and other violations of society's values.

This chapter concludes by examining GPM's Sustainable Project Principles which identify the key ethical considerations when managing and delivering projects, program, or portfolios as a modern professional.

PART TWO: The PRiSM Methodology

Notes

4. PRiSM Basics

PRiSM (PRojects integrating Sustainable Methods) was developed by GPM as a sustainability-centered project delivery approach to help manage the need to balance finite resources and social responsibility to achieve sustainable project outcomes. PRiSM helps organizations achieve their business objectives by helping them manage their projects efficiently and effectively in support of the Blue Economy model described in Section 1.2.

PRiSM is a structured project management approach that integrates sustainability with generally accepted project management practices to reduce negative environmental, social, and economic impacts in all types of projects. PRiSM is fully compatible with globally accepted standards related to professional project management such as ISO 21500, ISO 14001, ISO 26000, ISO 50001, and ISO 9001. See Chapters 0 and 0 for more detail on these and other standards that support sustainability.

As with other structured project management approaches (e.g., PRINCE2, Praxis, TenStep), PRiSM will require some amount of tailoring for most projects.

4.1. Project Management Concepts

4.1.1. What is a Project?

As noted in Section 2.1, GPM defines a project as "an investment that requires a set of coordinated activities performed over a finite period of time in order to accomplish a unique result in support of a desired outcome." To expand on the components of this definition:

- A *project* may be simple (making breakfast), complicated (design and construction of a commercial airport), or complex (development and implementation of an enterprise resource planning system).
- As an *investment*, each project requires a commitment of financial resources, non-financial resources, or both.
- *Coordinated* means that the work of the project is done in an organized way to ensure effective and efficient use of the committed resources.
- The *finite period of time* may be defined in advance as a constraint, determined by planning, or predicted through analysis of actual performance.
- *Unique* means that the characteristics of the result are different in some identifiable way.
- The *desired outcome* is expected to benefit one or more of the stakeholders.

The *activities*, the *period of time*, the *result*, and the *outcome* are typically described in general terms at the start of the project, then in more detail as the project progresses through the phases of the project lifecycle in-use. The PRiSM project lifecycle is described in Section 4.2.

4.1.2. What is Project Management?

Project management is the application of knowledge, skills, tools, and techniques to coordinate projects effectively and efficiently. Not all projects require project management. In particular, very simple projects (like breakfast) will not benefit from a documented business case, a risk register, or critical path analysis. At the opposite end of the spectrum, very large and very complex projects may require application of a program management approach.

Project management is a strategic competency for most organizations, enabling them to tie the project objectives to their business goals — and thus help improve their business results.

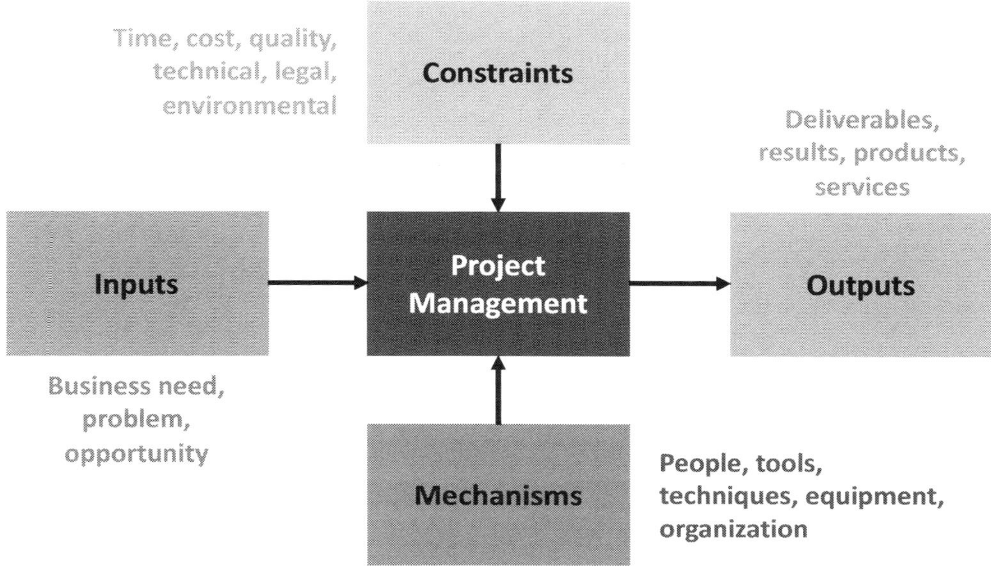

Figure 4-1: Project Management as a Process

Project management can be viewed as a process as illustrated above in Figure 4-1. The overall process of project management can also be viewed as a group of interconnected processes. These processes will fall into one of the following categories (adapted from ISO 21500):

- **Product-oriented processes** — are those used to specify and create the result of the project. They include processes for discovering customer requirements, designing a product or service, building physical artifacts, and other results as described in Section 4.3.
- **Project-management-oriented processes** — are those used to identify, describe, and organize project activities. They include processes for estimating, scheduling, risk identification, and others as described in Chapter 5.
- **Support-oriented processes** — are those used to support the other processes and are generally provided by organizational units outside the project. They normally include general management processes in fields such as procurement, logistics, finance, accounting, and safety. Common support processes are described in Chapter 6.

These processes are not always linear, and may be connected in different ways and in different sequences on different projects.

4.1.3. What is a Project Manager?

The *project manager* is the individual responsible for getting the project done. The project manager will normally be responsible for all of the resources, all of the activities, and all of the processes on a given project. Unless there are subprojects, there should only be one project manager for a project.

Section 2.4 contains additional information about the characteristics of a sustainable project manager.

4.1.4. Projects in the Organization

A project always exists within a larger organization that includes other activities. The larger organization is variously called the *performing organization*, the *permanent organization*, or the *stationary organization*. The other activities are typically called either *operations* or *business-as-usual* (BAU). In some cases, as with consulting or contracting firms, the other activities are other projects. Figure 4-2 below illustrates how projects fit within the larger organization.

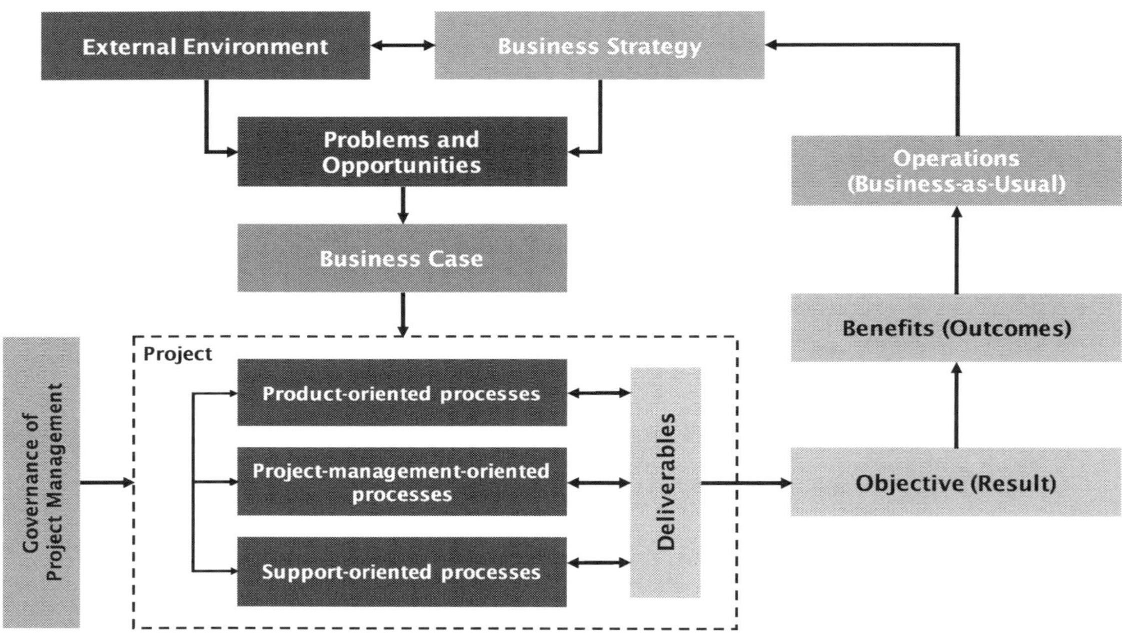

Figure 4-2: Project Environment (adapted from ISO 21500)

Problems and opportunities are identified by evaluating the impact of the organization's external environment on the organization's strategy. When a valid business case can be developed to solve a problem or take advantage of an opportunity, a project is approved.

The project is overseen according to the provisions of the organization's governance practices. Governance is covered in Chapter 7.

The project's processes produce the deliverables that are needed to satisfy the business case and to comply with the governance requirements. Those deliverables produce a result (or output) that satisfies the objective defined by the business case.

In use, the result of the project is used to realize benefits that support the organization's ongoing business activities.

4.2. PRiSM Project Lifecycle

Projects are usually divided into *phases* (also called *stages* or in some domains *iterations*) in order to provide better management control. The most fundamental characteristic of a project phase is that it ends with a decision about whether or not to continue:

- For most phases, the decision will be about whether or not to continue into the next phase. The key factor driving this decision should always be: is the business case still valid?
- For the project's final phase, the decision will be about whether or not to put the project's deliverables into use.

Phases follow a logical sequence designed to allow the project team to develop a deeper and more detailed understanding of the characteristics of the project objectives. Project phases are collectively known as the *project lifecycle.*

PRiSM is built around a standard project lifecycle designed to enhance sustainability in both the work and the results of the project. The project lifecycle is part of the cradle-to-cradle lifecycle described in Chapter 8.

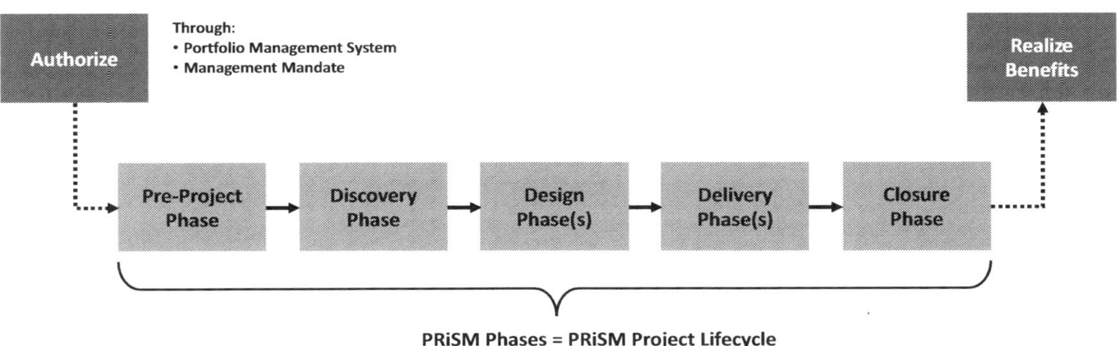

Figure 4-3: Overview Flowchart of the PRiSM Project Lifecycle

4.2.1. Pre-project Phase

The PRiSM *Pre-project Phase* is where the project objectives are identified, the project sponsor and project manager partnership is established, business case development begins, and prior lessons learned are reviewed.

Authorize. Authorizing a project involves formal approval to invest organizational resources in the project. This may come from a project portfolio management system or via a management mandate. Even the smallest project should be properly authorized.

Select Project Sponsor and Project Manager. The project sponsor is appointed by the project owner to provide overall guidance and support to the project and the project manager. The project manager is appointed to handle day-to-day responsibility for planning and managing the project.

Select Team for Business Case Development. For smaller, simpler projects, the business case "team" might include only the project sponsor, or perhaps the project sponsor and the project manager. For larger, more complex projects, additional resources will usually be required to help develop the business case.

Analyze Alternatives. The business case team should identify and analyze alternatives for the project objectives as well as alternatives for achieving those objectives. This analysis should take into consideration factors such as cost, schedule, expected benefits, risk, sustainability, resource availability, and resource capabilities.

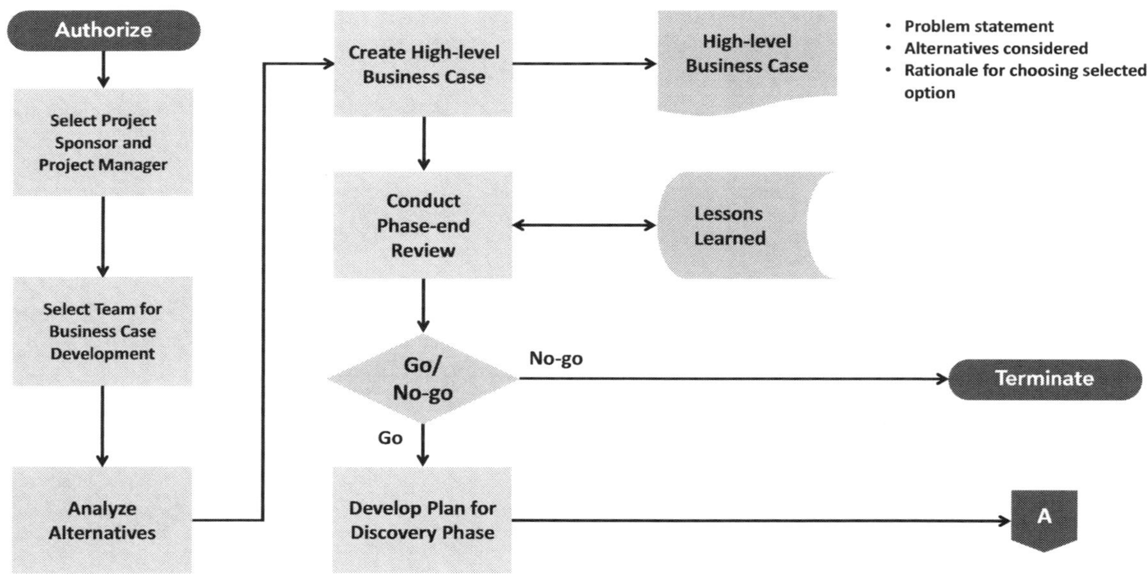

Figure 4-4: Pre-Project Phase Flowchart

Create High-level Business Case. The contents of the business case are discussed in more detail below in Section 4.3.1. In the Pre-Project Phase, there may not be enough detail available to develop more than a high-level business case that includes a problem statement (justification), brief descriptions of the alternatives considered, and the rationale for choosing the selected option.

Conduct Phase-End Review. At the end of each PRiSM phase, the project management team must evaluate what has been accomplished in the current phase in order to determine if the project should proceed to the next phase. The evaluation is done against the business case: is the project still necessary and useful?

Make Go/No-go Decision. The project sponsor will use the results of the phase-end review to decide whether to proceed to the next phase or to end the project.

Develop Plan for Discovery Phase. Once approval to proceed has been received, the project management team must develop a plan to guide the work of the Discovery Phase. The planning process is described in more detail in Chapter 5.

4.2.2. Discovery Phase

The PRiSM *Discovery Phase* is where requirements are defined, the business case is aligned to organizational systems, and sustainability impacts are identified, analyzed, and transformed into opportunities to create social, environmental, and economic value.

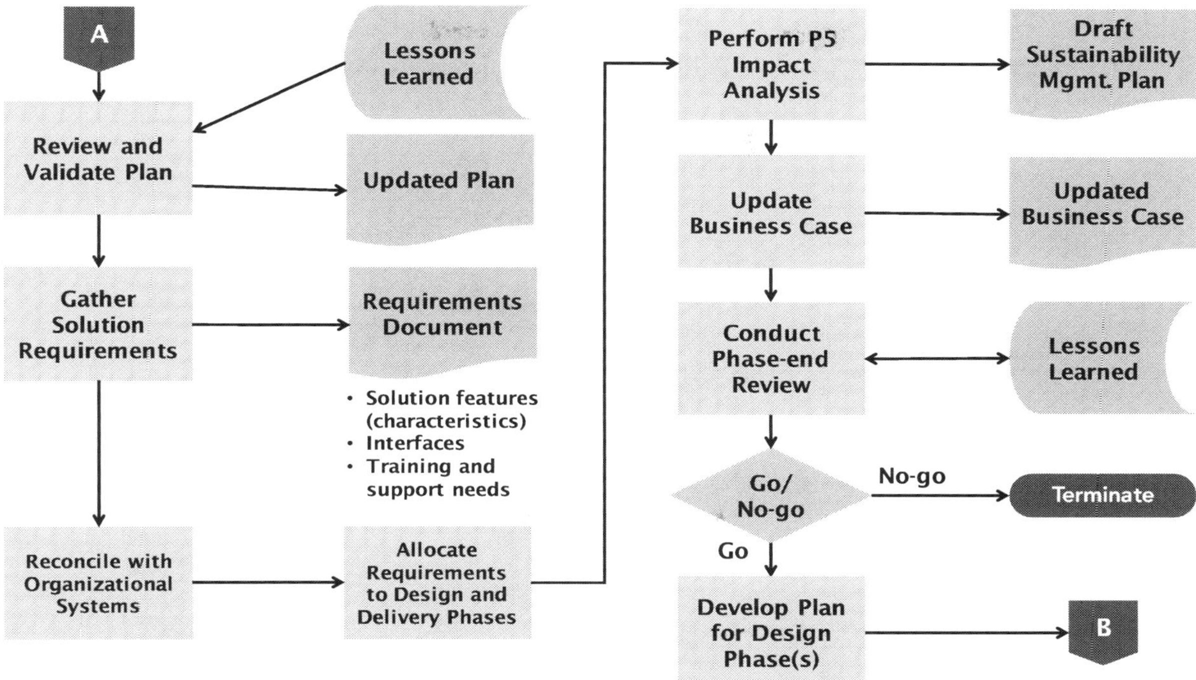

Figure 4-5: Discovery Phase Flowchart

Review and Validate Plan. The plan developed at the end of the previous phase should be reviewed by the team for the current phase to ensure that it remains useful and relevant. Delays in starting this phase or changes to staffing can have a significant impact.

Gather Solution Requirements. The process of gathering the information needed to complete a requirements document is described in Section 4.3.3.

Reconcile with Organizational Systems. This step involves balancing the project's objectives and plans with existing organizational systems.

Allocate Requirements to Design and Delivery Phases. This step involves determining which requirements will be addressed in each design and delivery phase.

Perform P5 Impact Analysis. Analyzing the solution and discovery processes against environmental, social, and economic criteria to ensure sustainable outcomes.

Update Business Case. Ensure that the business case remains valid.

Conduct Phase-End Review. At the end of each PRiSM phase, the project management team must evaluate what has been accomplished in the current phase in order to determine if the project should proceed to the next phase. The evaluation is done against the business case: is the project still necessary and useful?

Make Go/No-go Decision. The project sponsor will use the results of the phase-end review to decide whether to proceed to the next phase or to end the project.

Develop Plan for Design Phase(s). Once approval to proceed has been received, the project management team must develop a plan to guide the work of design. Design work may be planned as a single phase or as multiple, iterative phases. The planning process is described in more detail in Chapter 5.

4.2.3. Design Phase

The PRiSM *Design Phase* is where the solution is designed, the sustainability analysis is refined, and acceptance criteria are established. For larger, more complex projects, the Design Phase may be iterated.

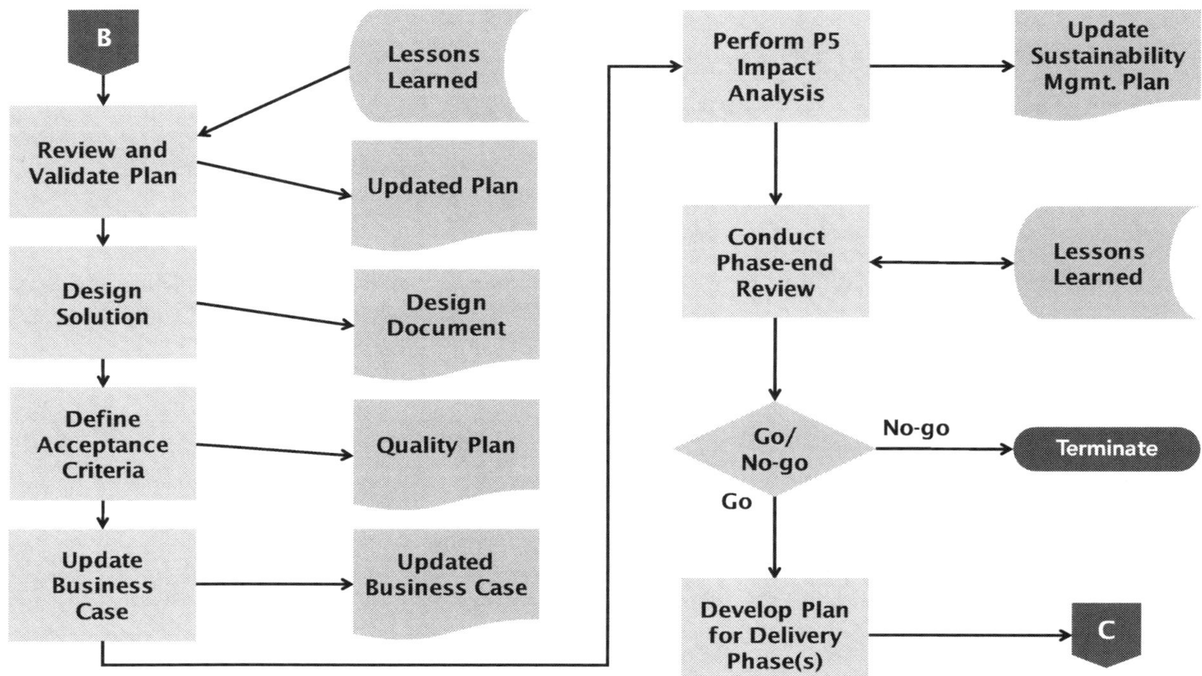

Figure 4-6: Design Phase Flowchart

Review and Validate Plan. The plan developed at the end of the previous phase should be reviewed by the team for the current phase to ensure that it remains useful and relevant. Delays in starting this phase or changes to staffing can have a significant impact.

Design Solution. The process of designing the product or service of the project by dividing it up into smaller components in order to determine resource needs, costs, schedule, risk, value, benefits, and impacts.

Define Acceptance Criteria. The process of documenting the criteria which must be satisfied before the project sponsor will approve the project deliverables.

Update Business Case. Ensure that the business case remains valid.

Perform P5 Impact Analysis. Re-analyzing the solution and analyzing design processes against environmental, social, and economic criteria to ensure sustainable outcomes.

Conduct Phase-End Review. At the end of each PRiSM phase, the project management team must evaluate what has been accomplished in the current phase in order to determine if the project should proceed to the next phase. The evaluation is done against the business case: is the project still necessary and useful?

Make Go/No-go Decision. The project sponsor will use the results of the phase-end review to decide whether to proceed to the next phase or to end the project.

Develop Plan for Delivery Phase(s). Once approval to proceed has been received, the project management team must develop a plan to guide delivery of the project solution. Delivery work may be planned as a single phase or as multiple, iterative phases. The planning process is described in more detail in Chapter 5.

4.2.4. Delivery Phase

The PRiSM *Delivery Phase* is where the project team produces the deliverables needed to achieve expected outcomes and benefits. For larger, more complex projects, the Delivery Phase may be iterated.

Review and Validate Plan. The plan developed at the end of the previous phase should be reviewed by the team for the current phase to ensure that it remains useful and relevant. Delays in starting this phase or changes to staffing can have a significant impact.

Develop Components. The process of making or buying the deliverables of the project.

Test Against Acceptance Criteria. The process of performing the test scenarios derived from the acceptance criteria to allow the project sponsor to make a decision about the project deliverables.

Update Business Case. Ensure that the business case remains valid.

Perform P5 Impact Analysis. Re-analyzing the solution and analyzing delivery processes against environmental, social, and economic criteria to ensure sustainable outcomes.

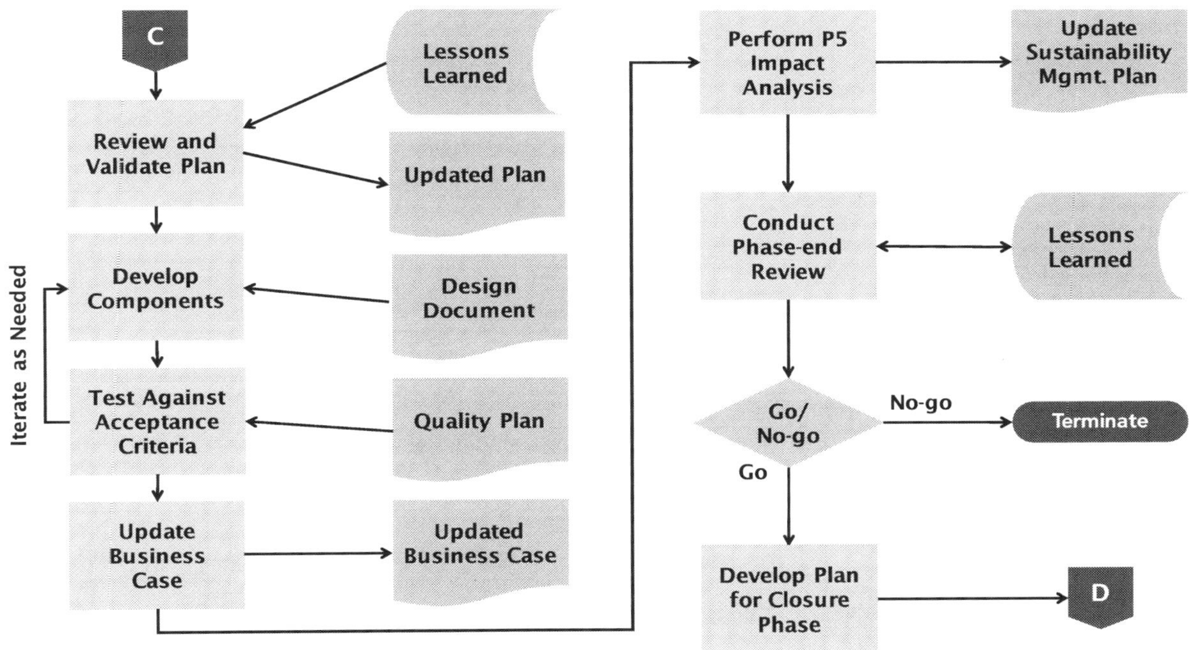

Figure 4-7: Delivery Phase Flowchart

Conduct Phase-End Review. At the end of each PRiSM phase, the project management team must evaluate what has been accomplished in the current phase in order to determine if the project should proceed to the next phase. The evaluation is done against the business case: is the project still necessary and useful?

Make Go/No-go Decision. The project sponsor will use the results of the phase-end review to decide whether to proceed to the next phase or to end the project.

Develop Plan for Closure Phase. Once approval to proceed has been received, the project management team must develop a plan to guide the activities required to close the project. The planning process is described in more detail in Chapter 5.

4.2.5. Closure Phase

The PRiSM *Closure Phase* is where the project team facilitates adoption of the project deliverables and administratively closes out the project.

Review and Validate Plan. The plan developed at the end of the previous phase should be reviewed by the team for the current phase to ensure that it remains useful and relevant. Delays in starting this phase or changes to staffing can have a significant impact.

Facilitate Acceptance and Adoption. This involves coordinating the handover of the deliverables to the relevant party and adoption into production. It may also include some level of support for ongoing operations and maintenance, organizational changes, and end-of-life planning.

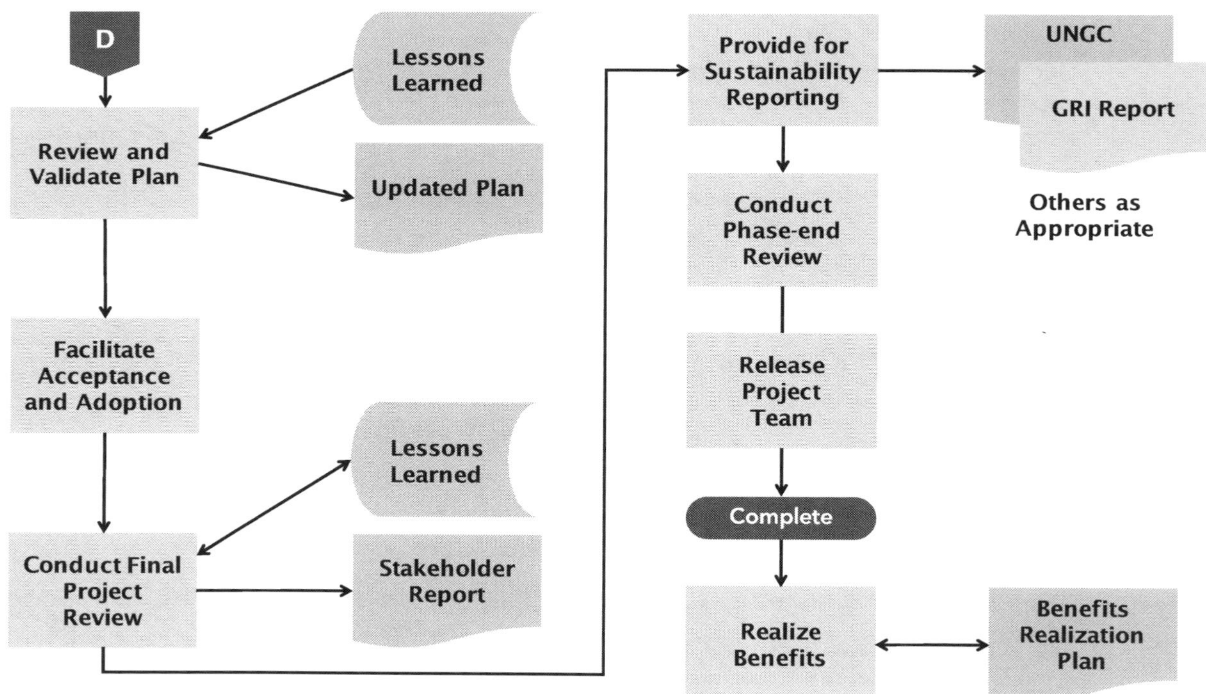

Figure 4-8: Closure Phase Flowchart

Conduct Final Project Review. The process performed with the project team to review elements of the project that were successful or unsuccessful.

Provide Information for Sustainability Reporting. Produce organizational materiality report from the Sustainability Management Plan to support sustainability reporting

Release Project Team. Formally release project team members from their project obligations.

Realize Benefits. Business benefits are realized as a result of the project.

4.2.6. Overview of Managing a PRiSM Project Lifecycle Phase

This topic is covered in detail in Chapter 5 with coverage of additional supporting activities included in Chapter 6. The chart below presents a high-level view.

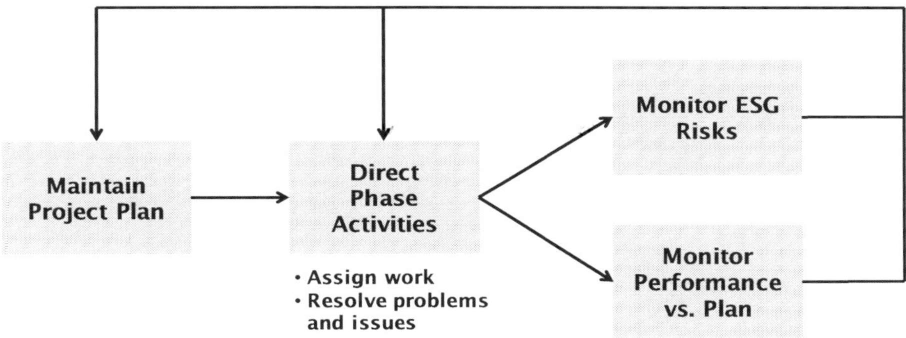

Figure 4-9: Flowchart of PRiSM Project Management Activities

Maintain Project Plan. The project plan should be updated at the end of each phase, and validated at the beginning of the next phase. This includes continued relevance as well as continued support for the business case. Project planning activities are detailed in Chapter 5.

Direct Phase Activities. This covers management of all of the phase's activities.

Monitor ESG Risks. In PRiSM projects, environmental, social, and governance risks merit special attention.

Monitor Performance vs. Plan. This includes taking remedial action when significant variances are discovered.

4.3. Key PRiSM Deliverables

4.3.1. Business Case

The *business case* documents *why* one particular project should be favored over others. The business case should explain how the project supports the strategy of the funding organization. It should contain enough information to enable a good decision about whether or not to fund the project. It should include at least:

- A description of the strategic fit: what strategic objectives the project supports and how.
- Documentation of the project objectives.

- A list and brief descriptions of the other options considered to demonstrate that the option chosen is the best option based on the information currently available. The list of options should generally include the option of deferring the project and of not doing it at all.
- Estimated costs and benefits.
- Product and project management success criteria.
- Acceptance criteria to be applied at the end of the project. In some cases, these will have to be developed during the project and added to the business case.

Most business cases will also include a high-level project plan covering:

- Major deliverables
- Key schedule targets
- Cost estimates
- Assumptions and constraints
- Primary risks

Additional planning detail will be developed as the project proceeds through the phases of the PRiSM Project Lifecycle. Additional detail that has a significant effect on the business case should be incorporated into the business case.

In addition to being the primary support for project approval, the business case also provides important input to:

- Phase end reviews
- Evaluating change requests
- Lessons learned
- Verification of expected benefits

4.3.2. *P5 Impact Analysis*

The *P5 Impact Analysis* (see Figure 4-10) is a summary of the steps that will be taken by the project team to decrease negative sustainability impacts and to increase positive ones. It is based on the P5 Standard discussed in Section 2.3.

The primary purpose of this document is to ensure that the project team members and other key stakeholders remain alert to what could affect the project's impact on sustainability. The P5 Standard provides a checklist of topics to consider, and the impact analysis itself is similar to a risk register for sustainability.

The P5 Impact Analysis is usually best done in a workshop to encourage awareness and understanding.

P5 Classification			Description	Potential Impact	Impact Score	Proposed Action
Sub-Category	**Element**	**Area**				
Social Impacts (People)						
1. Labor Practices and Decent Work	d. Training and Education	Process	Proposed components are all simple to construct	Most work can be done by low-skilled laborers	+1	Schedule paid training day for workers
2. Society and Customer	c. Customer Health and Safety	Process	Playground is near two elementary schools	Children access the worksite and get injured	-3	Enclose worksite with security fence
					+2	Educate community about worksite hazards
Environmental Impacts (Planet)						
5. Transport	a. Logistics	Process	Many companies provide the products and services that will be needed	Remote suppliers will consume more fuel and generate more pollution	-2	Give bonus points in selection process to local suppliers
6. Energy	a. Energy Consumption	Process/ Product	Energy costs exceed approved budget	Project has to de-scope	-2	Use energy efficient tools and materials
6. Energy	d. Renewable Energy	Product	Lighting will be a major operating cost	Reduced operating hours	+2	Use solar panels as energy source
Economic Impacts (Prosperity)						
11. Economic Stimulation	d. Indirect Benefits	Product	No other restrooms in vicinity of new park	Limited access could cause vandalism	+1	Allow use by those not using park facilities

Figure 4-10: Extract from P5 Impact Analysis

The contents of a P5 Impact Analysis can also be used to analyze design options as illustrated in Figure 4-11 below. This chart shows the average ratings for each of three different implementation options.

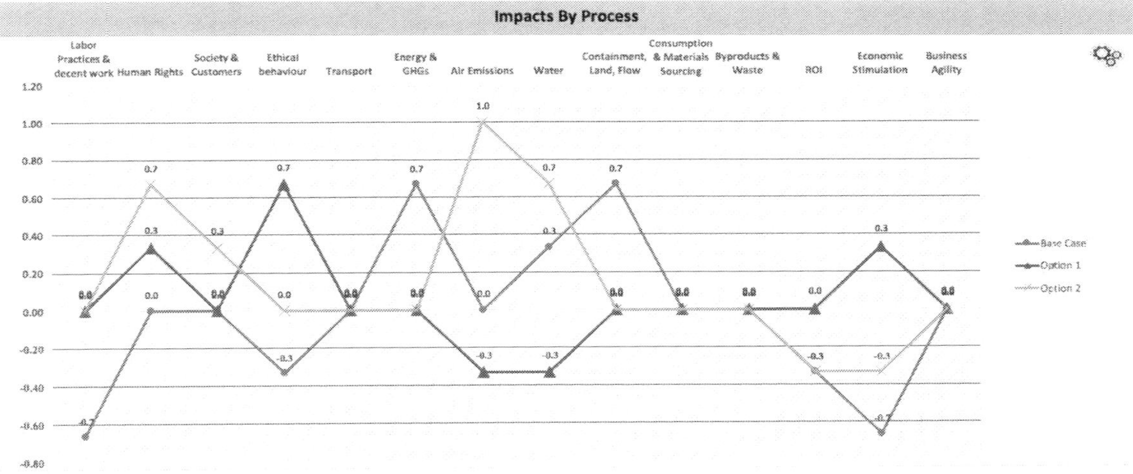

Figure 4-11: P5 Impact Analysis Report Example

4.3.3. Requirements Document

The *requirements document* describes the externally visible functions and attributes of the various deliverables. The fact that a requirement must be externally visible also implies that it must be possible to test any requirement. The ways to elicit and document requirements varies by domain, but in general, if something is needed to satisfy the project's objective, it is a requirement.

The requirements documents should be verified against the business case to ensure that the specified requirements are consistent with the project objectives.

The requirements document is maintained throughout the project in response to new requirements, changed requirements, and clarified requirements.

Requirements will generally fall into one of the following categories:

- **Sustainability requirements.** Descriptions of what the project must do or deliver in order to be considered *sustainable*.
- **User requirements.** Descriptions of the needs of a particular stakeholder or group of stakeholders. They usually describe how to interact with the intended solution.
- **Functional requirements.** Descriptions of specific capabilities, behavior, and information that the solution will need.
- **Non-functional requirements.** Descriptions of the conditions under which the solution must remain effective such as reliability, testability, and maintainability.
- **Implementation requirements.** Descriptions of capabilities or behavior required to enable transition from the current state of the funding organization to the desired future state.

The Requirements Document is the major input into the design phase(s). It is also an important input into the verification process since tests should trace back to specific requirements.

It allows stakeholders to understand *what* the project's deliverables should do without defining *how* they should do it.

4.3.4. Design Document

The *Design Document* describes the physical aspects of how the deliverables will be created. For complex deliverables, there may be multiple levels of design such as a conceptual design followed by a detailed design. The Design Document may include sketches, flowcharts, and calculations as well as narrative material.

As with the Requirements Document, the contents and structure will vary by domain. Many organizations will have templates.

The design document is a living document that is updated throughout the project in response to new requirements, changed requirements, clarified requirements, and new information from either the design or delivery activities.

4.3.5. Sustainability Management Plan

The *Sustainability Management Plan* (SMP) is one of several management plans (see Section 5.7) that describe and document how the sustainability aspects of the project will be managed. The SMP describes how the project management team plans to balance the often-conflicting needs of economic, environmental, and social responsibility.

The SMP will normally cover at least the following topics:

- **Key Performance Indicators (KPIs).** These will be as outlined in the P5 Impact Analysis.
- **Environmental impact assessment.** A summary of the planned environmental impact and steps that will be taken to decrease the effects or increase the opportunities identified.
- **Scope Exclusions.** Any known areas of potential sustainability impact that the project will not address.

- **Sustainability risk management.** Any differences from standard practices in the approach to identifying, analyzing, and responding to sustainability risks.
- **Reviews and reporting.** Steps to take in a project audit regarding sustainability and how sustainability metrics will be reported throughout the project.

The SMP document should also include the following:

- **P5 Impact Assessment.** A snapshot of the project's P5 score and incremental re-baselining from previous assessments. It should include recommended actions to be taken in order to increase benefits and mitigate risks.
- **Approvals and Signoffs Page.** A section to gain approval for the project manager to take action based on the P5 impact assessment.
- **Sustainability Reporting Summary.** A description of how the project and its outcomes contribute to the organization's sustainability strategy and utilized as material for sustainability reporting.

Note: organizations that are committed to sustainability will usually have a Sustainability Management Plan at the executive level as well as SMPs for each project.

The *GPM P5 Standard for Sustainability in Project Management* is a stand-alone document. The standard outlines the process for performing a P5 impact analysis. You can download the standard at http://www.greenprojectmanagement.org/p5.

4.3.6. Project Success Criteria

Project success has traditionally been defined in terms of completing the project within cost, schedule, and scope constraints as illustrated below.

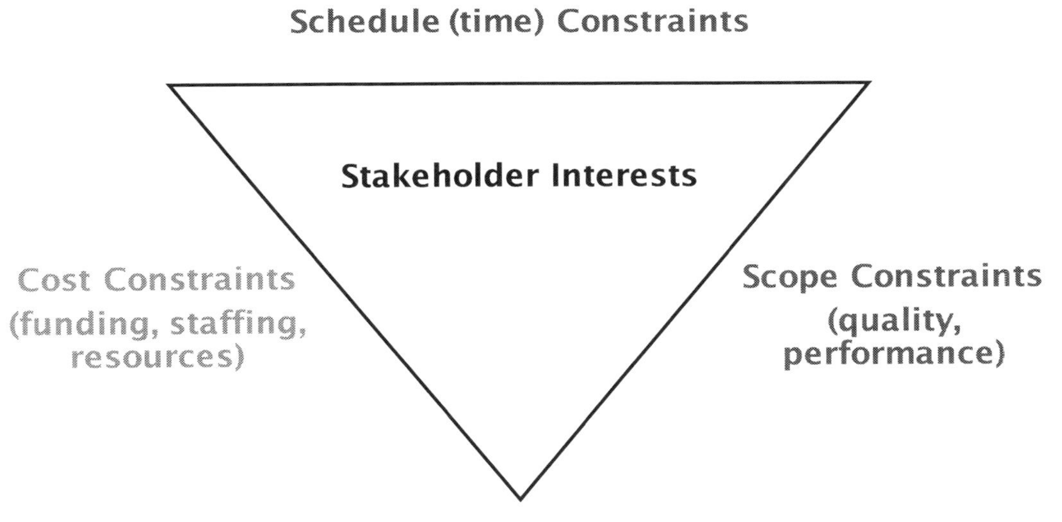

Figure 4-12: A Modern View of the Triple Constraint

On occasion, quality and stakeholder satisfaction have been called out separately rather than being subsumed within scope. This concept was often called the *Triple Constraint* or the *Iron Triangle*. The common theme in all cases was that project success was defined:

- In ways that could be measured the day the project was finished.
- Using measures that were mostly under the control of the project team.

But what about the Sydney Opera House? It cost somewhere around *sixteen* times as much to build and took at least *twice* as long to complete as the original estimates. Yet it is an enduring and inspiring civic symbol. Was that project really a failure?

The Sydney Opera House illustrates that project success has two dimensions:

- Product success — were the expected benefits realized?
- Project management success — was the project well-managed?

Simple yes-or-no answers will not suffice since different stakeholders will have different answers. With PRiSM, we no longer ask, "was this project a success?" Instead, we ask, "how successful was this project along each dimension?" (See Section 4.3.6)

Structured Success Criteria

To ensure useful project success criteria, PRiSM uses a structured format. For example, here's an example of a structured statement for schedule success:

- Measurable item: "the completion date of every major milestone"
- Comparison statement: "must be within"
- Some number: "one week of the baseline schedule date"

Each project is unique, so here are some other examples of schedule success criteria:

- All work completed by the original agreed date.
- All priority functions fully-tested and ready for release prior to the announced release date.
- Receipt of an occupancy permit by November 15, 2018.

Product Success Criteria

Most of the potential product success measures such as reduced carbon footprint, operational improvements, revenue increases, and cost savings are usually beyond the direct control of the project team and are not measurable until well after the project is finished.

But the project management team still needs to know what these measures are so it can make good decisions in support of them. For example, if one of the measures of product success for a software development project is to reduce maintenance costs by 50%, the team might choose to shorten the time for parallel operations in order to satisfy that criterion.

Project Management Success Criteria

All projects should have at least four measures of project management success — one each for cost, schedule, and scope, and another for stakeholder satisfaction. Larger projects may have more, but four is the minimum. One aspect of stakeholder satisfaction is attainment of sustainability objectives during the project.

Criteria for Good Success Criteria

As with any other tool or technique, project success measures can be overdone. Use the following checklist to help ensure that your measures are good measures. They should be:

- **Complete** — anything unmeasured is likely to be compromised.
- **Relevant** — variances clearly indicate a need for corrective action.
- **Valid** — measuring what you intended to measure.
- **Easy to understand** — so that people will accept them.
- **Economical to obtain** — know the value of the information.

4.4. Summary

This chapter introduces the PRiSM methodology and provides an overview of the key elements and the PRiSM project lifecycle. PRiSM has been developed to ensure that the project management approach as well as the project outputs are sustainable.

PRiSM includes five phases, two of which, design and delivery, may be repeated multiple times depending on the nature of the work being done.

By following the PRiSM lifecycle and producing the key PRiSM deliverables, P5 impacts can be identified, measured, and managed and anticipated benefits can be delivered.

PRiSM can be used in any sector and in any organization. While elements of PRiSM may be similar to other approaches, the P5 Impact Assessment and Sustainability Management Plan are key differentiators. By combining these two items with proven practices from traditional project management, PRiSM help to ensure that projects deliver sustainable outcomes in a sustainable way.

5. Managing a PRiSM Project Lifecycle Phase

This chapter describes the activities used to manage the creation of the deliverables described in the previous chapter. For most projects, each phase of the project lifecycle will require repeating each activity. However, the amount of effort required for each will vary significantly.

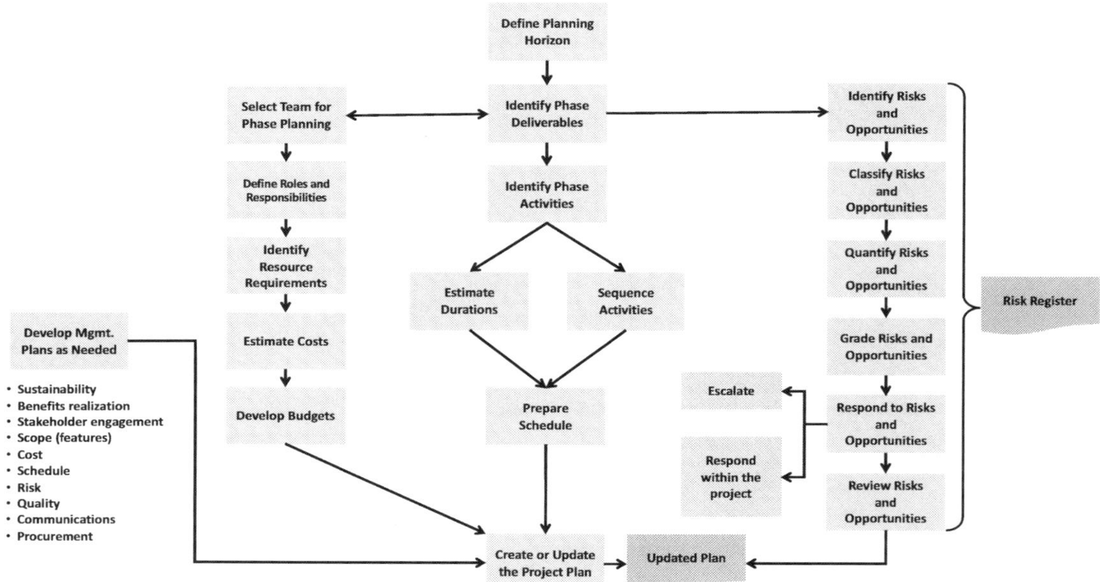

Figure 5-1: Flowchart of Project Management Activities in PRiSM

5.1. Basic Planning

Plans are statements of intent: they define what the project is intended to achieve and how to achieve it. Plans will be larger and more complex for larger and more complex projects. Plans are expected to change in response to new information and changing circumstances.

5.1.1. Define Planning Horizon

The first activity requires determining how far into the future to plan. In general, you should plan at least through the end of the upcoming phase. If that is not feasible, the planning horizon should focus on how to get the information required to allow planning through the end of the upcoming phase.

The planning horizon may be extended if all of the following conditions are met:

- This project is similar to others that the team members have completed successfully before.
- You have reliable historical data to support accurate budgeting and scheduling decisions.
- The project's risk profile is within acceptable limits for the funding organization (i.e., project failure would not bankrupt it).

5.1.2. Create or Update the Project Plan

This activity can be performed in parallel with the other project management activities, or it can be the final step in the planning process.

The project plan is a comprehensive set of documents that provides the guidance needed to manage the project. It includes, but is not limited to, the budget, the schedule, identified risks and risk responses, team roles and responsibilities, and the management plans described in Section 5.7.

Access to the project plan will vary based on the structure of the project team. Proprietary information may need to be protected, and there could be individual privacy issues, but in general, PRiSM assumes widespread availability.

5.2. Staffing and Personnel

The activities described below may include individuals and groups both internal and external to the performing organization. They should always include anyone who contributes directly to the completion of a project deliverable.

5.2.1. Select Team for Phase Planning

As with many other aspects of project management, who needs to be involved with phase planning will vary based on the phase and the nature of the work to be planned. Larger and more complex projects may need several levels of planning teams. Subject matter expertise is almost always required to support planning.

5.2.2. Define Roles and Responsibilities

Defining roles and responsibilities requires answering several basic questions:

- Who is going to report to whom about what?
- Who will be responsible for creating, reviewing, and approving project deliverables?

Roles are usually documented in a Communications Management Plan as described in Section 5.7. Responsibilities are generally documented using an Organization Breakdown Structure (OBS), a Responsibility Assignment Matrix (RAM), or both. There are two main differences between an OBS and a RAM:

- An OBS includes reporting relationships; a RAM does not.
- A RAM includes what each individual or group is responsible for by deliverable; an OBS does not.

In both cases, the source for the deliverables should be either the Work Breakdown Structure (WBS) or Product Breakdown Structure (PBS) to ensure that all items have been included.

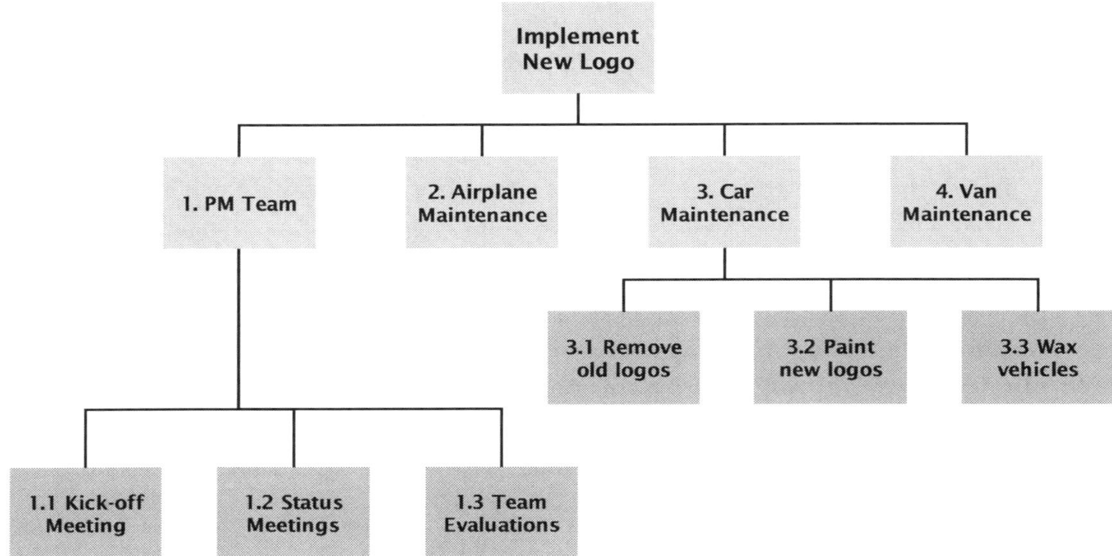

Figure 5-2: Upper Levels of an Organizational Breakdown Structure

There are many varieties of RAM, usually named after the coding used to describe responsibilities. These include PARIS (illustrated below), RACI (Responsible, Accountable, Consulted, Informed), RASCI (RACI plus Support), and others. A RAM may also be called a Linear Responsibility Matrix.

Team Member ➔ / Deliverable ↓	Sponsor	Project Manager	Educator #1	Educator #1	Designer	Support Staff
1.1 Course outline	A	R	P	S		
2.1 Course content	I	A	P	S	R	
2.2 Graphic elements	I	A			P	
2.3 Participant activities	I	A	S	P		
3.1 Assessment tool	A	R		P		
4.1 Pilot offering	I	A				P

P = Primary A = Approval R = Reviewer I = Information S = Secondary

Figure 5-3: Partial Example of an Responsibility Assignment Matrix

5.3. Deliverables

Deliverables are the physical artifacts that the project produces. They will include management deliverables (status reports, updated project plans, etc.), interim product descriptions (requirements document, design document, etc.), and final products and services (software, buildings, etc.).

5.3.1. *Identify Phase Deliverables*

Phase deliverables are generally identified through either a Product Breakdown Structure (PBS) or a Work Breakdown Structure (WBS).

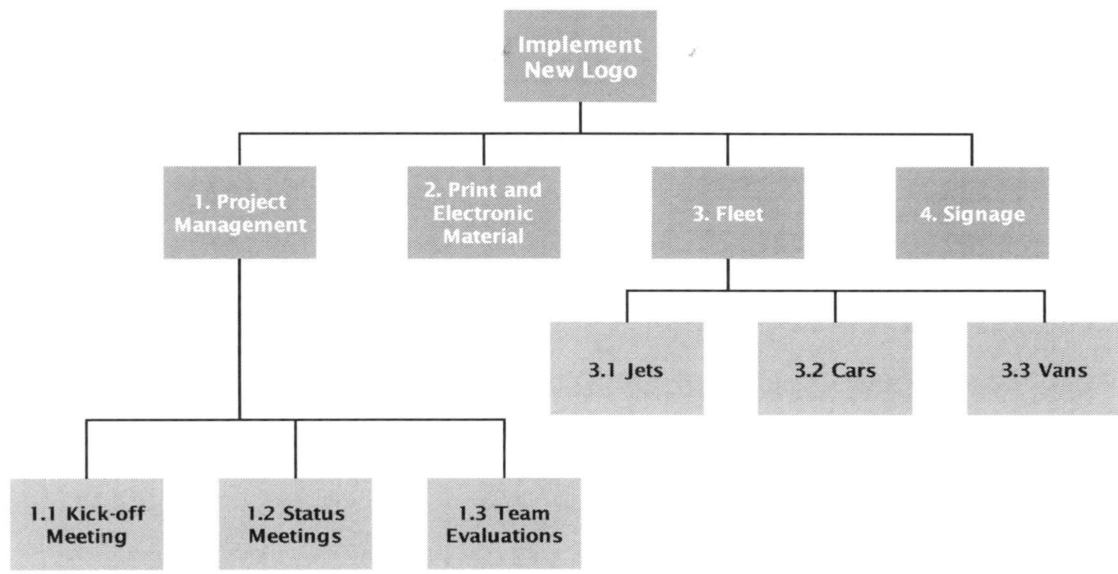

Figure 5-4: Upper Levels of a Work Breakdown Structure

A WBS is a hierarchical breakdown of the components that will be delivered to satisfy the project objectives (see figure above). As with any breakdown, the lower levels provide more detail about the higher levels. In a WBS, every item is described as a noun (a *thing*). The acceptance criteria for each item are included in a supplementary document.

Some authors mistakenly argue that the items in a WBS should be described using a verb (making each box an *action*). This is incorrect as can readily be determined by examining any recognized project management standard that describes the use of the WBS.

A PBS is also a hierarchical breakdown of the components that will be delivered to satisfy the project objectives. Both breakdown structures should have a numbering system as illustrated to allow clear reference to each element.

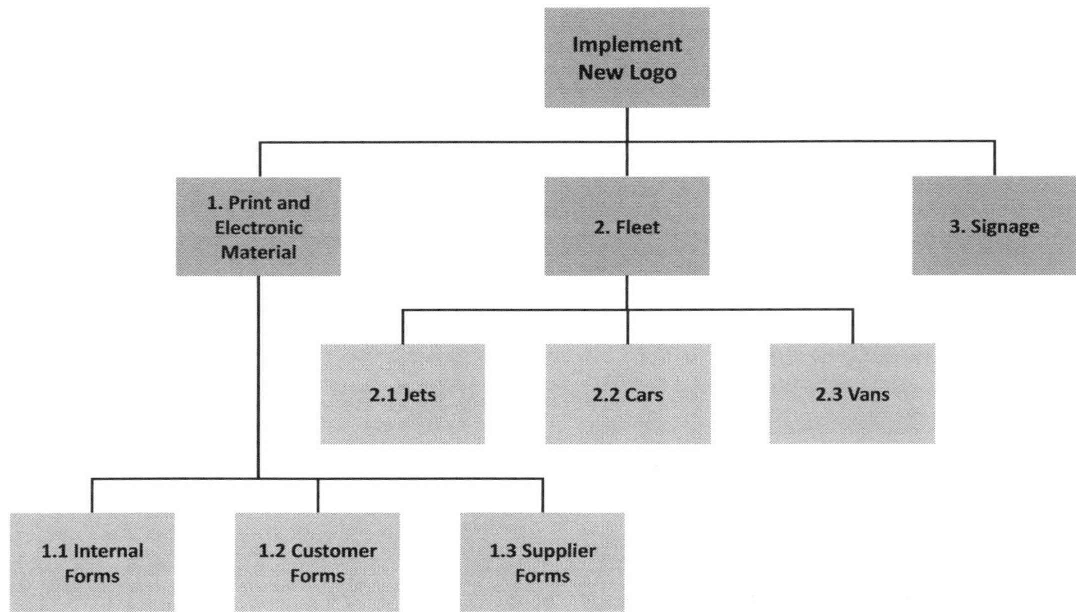

Figure 5-5: Upper Levels of a Product Breakdown Structure

The main difference between a PBS and a WBS is that the WBS includes a branch for management activities (review meetings, status reports, etc.) while a PBS does not.

Neither a PBS nor a WBS is normally developed for the Pre-Project Phase: a simple list is usually adequate to define the deliverables for that phase. If the output of the project is well-understood, it may be possible to develop a reasonably complete PBS or WBS for the balance of the project during the Discovery Phase. For most projects, the coverage of either the PBS or the WBS will be limited to the current phase.

Deliverables should have *acceptance criteria* defined and agreed as soon as possible (but no sooner). Project stakeholders must be made aware that changes to acceptance criteria will almost always affect both budget and schedule.

Acceptance criteria are used to determine if the project has delivered what was requested. They must be measurable and unambiguous. They must be achievable within the constraints of the project.

5.3.2. *Identify Phase Activities*

Each deliverable requires two or more *activities* for its completion. By convention, activities are not included in either the PBS or WBS even though they represent an additional level of breakdown.

For large, complex projects, it may be necessary to create additional levels of detail before defining activities. Additional detail may be required to provide:

- Single-point responsibility for each deliverable
- Sufficient detail to estimate both costs and duration
- Smaller or shorter activities for progress reporting

External contracting — the possibility of controlling external work through contracts — can reduce the need for detailed breakdowns. In this way, areas of the PBS/WBS can be "blocked off" and allocated to the contractor for their own structure to be developed.

5.4. Risks and Opportunities

Risks and opportunities are present in all projects as a consequence of uncertainty: more things can happen than will happen. Risks are possible future events that could have a negative impact on the project while opportunities are possible future events that could have a positive impact.

Throughout the risk and opportunity management process, sustainable project managers should keep in mind:

- Different organizations and different individuals will find different levels of risk acceptable. For example, some people find roller coasters exhilarating while others find them terrifying.
- Almost all of the numbers used in analyzing both risks and opportunities are estimates with varying ranges of uncertainty. In some cases, estimates of probability and impact will be little more than informed guesses.
- Impacts, particularly negative impacts like the loss of life, often have an intangible component that can be hard to factor into the decision-making process.
- Research (Kahneman, 2011) has shown that most individuals are not good at estimating either probabilities or impacts due to factors such as confirmation bias.

5.4.1. *Identify Risks and Opportunities*

Tools commonly used to *identify risks and opportunities* include:

- **Risk and opportunity checklists** — are domain-specific lists of risks and opportunities that have occurred on previous projects. Many organizations have risk and opportunity checklists that they have developed themselves, and the web is an excellent resource as well.
- **P5 Impact Analysis** — is a sustainability risk assessment intended to analyze the project's product and process impacts across social, environmental, and economic domains.
- **Environmental impact assessment** — is similar to a risk checklist in that it is intended to ensure that all reasonable possibilities have been considered. Environmental scans may be structured or unstructured. One of the more popular structured approaches is called PESTLE which asks the team to consider political, economic, social, technological, legal, and environmental factors.
- **Interviews** — with stakeholders or subject matter experts can elicit ideas that the project team may not have considered.
- **Lessons learned** — are historical records from previous projects, especially similar projects, and can be an excellent source of ideas about future events that could affect this project.
- **Brainstorming** — is an interactive, open format group method to identify risks and opportunities.
- **Assumptions analysis** — all assumptions and constraints can be converted into risk or opportunity statements.

A risk register should be opened at the start of the project, and new risks and opportunities should be recorded as they arise. The risk register (typically, a spreadsheet) documents basic information about each item:

- Cause and effect (*effect* is also called *impact*)
- Probability of occurrence
- Planned response (see Section 5.4.5 below)
- Owner

The risk or opportunity owner is the person responsible for monitoring events to determine if the planned response should be implemented, or if the estimated probabilities and effects have changed.

5.4.2. *Classify Risks and Opportunities*

The first step in classifying risks and opportunities is to determine whether to manage the identified potential event as a risk or an opportunity since most events can be described as either. For example:

- Risk: key staff may become unavailable before the project is over.
- Opportunity: retaining key staff will help meet budget and schedule targets

The next step is to document the components of the potential future event:

- **Cause** — also called *driver* or *source*. This is the situation that allows the uncertainty to exist. For example, *staff turnover* is a source of risk.
- **Event** — the specific event that might arise from the source. For example, if the project's lead engineer gets a new job, that would be a risk event.
- **Effect** — how the event will affect the project's objectives.

5.4.3. *Quantify Risks and Opportunities*

Quantifying risks and opportunities involves documenting absolute or relative values for the event characteristics that will be used to grade the identified risks and opportunities. Event characteristics always include probability of occurrence and magnitude of effect. They may also include proximity, frequency, and vividness.

Absolute values for effects are usually given in monetary units. Relative values are usually given as a point on a rating scale as illustrated in the next section.

5.4.4. *Grade Risks and Opportunities*

The most common way to grade risks and opportunities is with a Probability-Impact matrix (P-I matrix) as shown below in Figure 5-6. A P-I matrix can be 5x5 as shown or 3x3 if the additional granularity is unlikely to be useful.

The color coding shown here is typical, but not universal. For example, some organizations make all high impact risks red for all levels of probability.

When using a P-I matrix, the ratings should not be multiplied or added since the results of those calculations lack meaning. For example, a result of 20 (5 x 4) does not mean that the risk in that cell is twice as bad as a risk with a result of 10 (2 x 5). In fact, as illustrated in the figure, a result of 5 x 1 may not be rated the same as one with a score of 1 x 5.

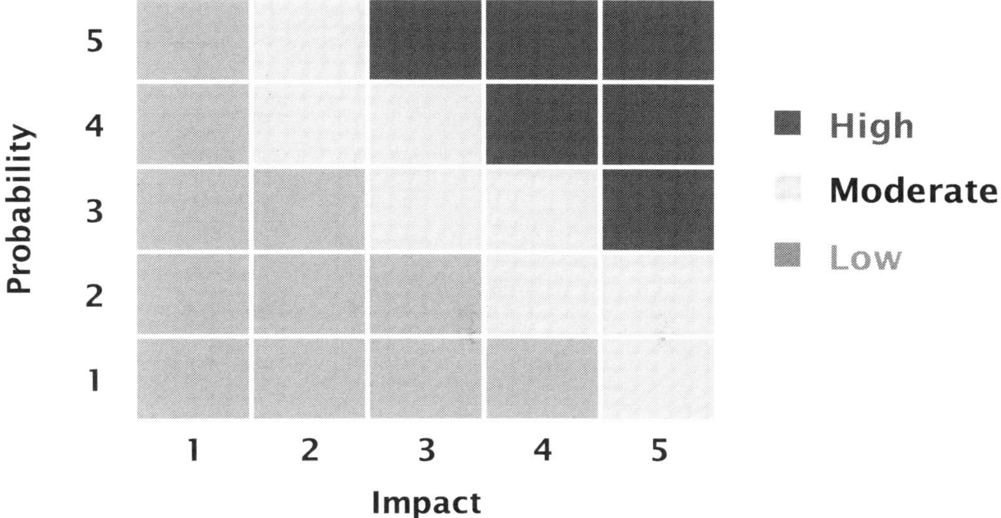

Figure 5-6: Probability-Impact Matrix

Each "score" represents a range that must be defined. For example, in the matrix above, a high cost impact (5) may be greater than $500,000; medium (3) from $100,000 to $250,000; and low impact (1) less than $50,000. Each risk or opportunity is placed on the matrix based on its estimated probability and impact with its placement determining how the team should respond to it.

5.4.5. *Respond to Risks and Opportunities*

Response plans can be developed and implemented once the risks have been assessed and graded. There are a number of generic response strategies:

- **Mitigate** — do something to reduce the probability, the impact, or both. Contingency plans and cost and schedule reserves are common mitigation approaches.
- **Accept** — this is the response of choice for low probability, low impact risks. Acceptance means that the team will do nothing unless and until the risk becomes a problem.
- **Transfer** — shift responsibility to an organization better placed to manage the risk. Most contracting is done in order to transfer common risks to the contractor.
- **Avoid** — a change in strategy or approach may allow the team to avoid the risk completely. Avoidance means that the risk cannot affect the project in any way: either the probability or impact is reduced to zero.
- **Escalate** — pass the risk up the management chain if the team lacks the ability to respond.

Responses to opportunities include:

- **Exploit** — do something to ensure that the opportunity can be realized.
- **Enhance** — do something to increase the probability or the impact that the opportunity can be realized.
- **Share** — shift the responsibility for trying to enhance the opportunity to another party. Where transference usually involves an outside party, sharing is normally done within the organization.
- **Ignore** — do nothing in advance to take advantage of the opportunity.

Response plans are developed after the risks and opportunities have been graded. Responses should be recorded in the risk register.

5.4.6. *Review Risks and Opportunities*

Risks and opportunities should be reviewed regularly to identify changes to previously identified items as well as to identify new ones. Both changed items and new items should be prioritized and responded to.

When a risk or opportunity is realized (when the potential event actually occurs), either the planned response is executed or a response is developed if the risk was accepted or the opportunity ignored.

5.5. Cost and Finance

Cost is about how much money can be spent for the project while *finance* is about securing the funds to be spent. On most projects, the project manager only needs to manage cost. On some projects, such as grant-funded projects, they may also need to worry about finance. However, since finance is mostly managed by the project sponsor, we'll focus on cost in this section.

When projects are done under contract, *price* (how much the supplier charges the customer) is also a consideration that may affect project management decisions. The supplier's price can be greater than or less than the supplier's cost.

5.5.1. *Identify Resource Requirements*

In order to *identify resource requirements*, we start by analyzing the project's deliverables and activities. This activity is focused on identifying what kinds of resources will be required: *estimate costs* below is about identifying how much of each type of resource will be required.

Major Categories	Subcategories
Consumables	Raw materials, money (funding), natural resources
Non-consumables	Machinery, technology, facilities, equipment, people, knowledge

Table 5-1: Resource Categories

5.5.2. Estimate Costs

An *estimate* is an informed assessment of an uncertain event. *Informed* means that you have an identified basis for the estimate. *Uncertain* recognizes that multiple outcomes are possible. Estimates are expressed as ranges. Estimating is covered in more depth in Section 6.2.

Cost is a measure of resource usage — employees and contractors must be paid, equipment must be bought or rented, and so on. Cost is usually expressed in monetary terms (dollars, euros, yuan, etc.), but it can also be expressed in terms of hours of effort. Using monetary units instead of effort hours makes it easier to compare estimates within or across projects.

Cost estimating includes identifying and considering alternatives. For example, if you need a hole in the ground for a building's foundation, you may be able to dig that hole with a bulldozer, a backhoe, or a steam shovel.

When preparing cost estimates, you should also document the assumptions behind them to facilitate later analysis if the estimates prove inaccurate. Costs are normally estimated for each resource required to complete the deliverable or activity.

5.5.3. Develop Budgets

A *budget* provides a management control to be used to track project progress. Unlike a cost estimate which is always a range, a cost budget is a single number. Cost budgets should be based on the cost estimates with higher budgets for more uncertain estimates. Many projects will have separate budgets for tracking different categories of costs (e.g., risk responses) or to satisfy the information needs of some stakeholders (e.g., cashflow).

For most projects, the cost budgets will be developed bottom-up: budgets will be developed for the lowest level of planning detail, then summed to obtain a project budget as illustrated in the table below:

Deliverable	Activity	Activity Budgets	Summed Budgets
Project Total			1,155
Item 1			700
	Activity 1.1	100	↑
	Activity 1.2	200	
	Activity 1.3	250	
	Activity 1.4	150	
Item 2			455
	Activity 2.1	125	↑
	Activity 2.2	135	
	Activity 2.3	195	

Table 5-2: Bottom-up Budget Development

Budgets may also be displayed graphically. In the chart below, the project has been divided into months, and the amounts budgeted are shown in the chart: the green bars represent monthly budgets and the blue line shows cumulative numbers.

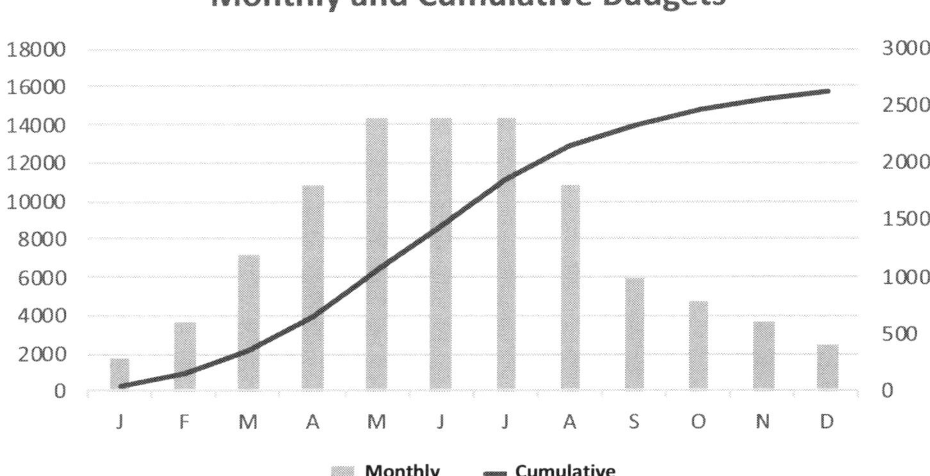

Figure 5-7: Monthly and Cumulative Project Budgets

The cumulative numbers typically take the shape of a stretched letter "s" and are commonly referred to as an "s-curve." In addition to the total project budget shown here, s-curves may be generated for cashflow or other cost categories.

Larger projects may also require the creation of a Cost Breakdown Structure (CBS). The CBS sums the detail budget items by cost category as shown below.

Deliverable	Activity	Activity Budgets	Summed Budgets
Project Total			1,075
Labor			575
	Activity 1.1	200	
	Activity 1.2	100	
	Activity 2.1	100	
	Activity 2.2	175	
Materials			500
	Activity 1.1	200	
	Activity 2.2	300	

Table 5-3: Cost Breakdown Structure

5.6. Time and Schedule

The schedule is of major importance on most projects, and sustainable projects are no different. Time can be of paramount importance when it comes to responding to natural disasters or taking action to reduce an organization's carbon footprint.

5.6.1. Estimate Durations

As with estimating costs, *estimating durations* involves making informed assessments of uncertain events. Estimates are again expressed as ranges. Estimating is covered in more depth in Section 6.2.

The default assumption for estimating durations is to use the duration that produces the lowest cost. If necessary, this assumption can be modified as part of preparing a schedule. Other assumptions which may affect duration estimates include:

- Resource productivity (resource availability is addressed as part of preparing a schedule)
- The impact of team size if multiple individuals will be involved

Durations are estimated at the most detailed level available, then summed using network analysis to determine the project schedule.

5.6.2. Sequence Activities

In order to *sequence activities*, the planning team must examine the WBS for dependencies: which activities must be done first, what can then be done next, and so on until all activities have been linked. Sequencing can also be done back-to-front: what is the final deliverable, what must be finished before it can be finished, and so on back to the start.

Sequences are typically captured in a network logic diagram as illustrated below.

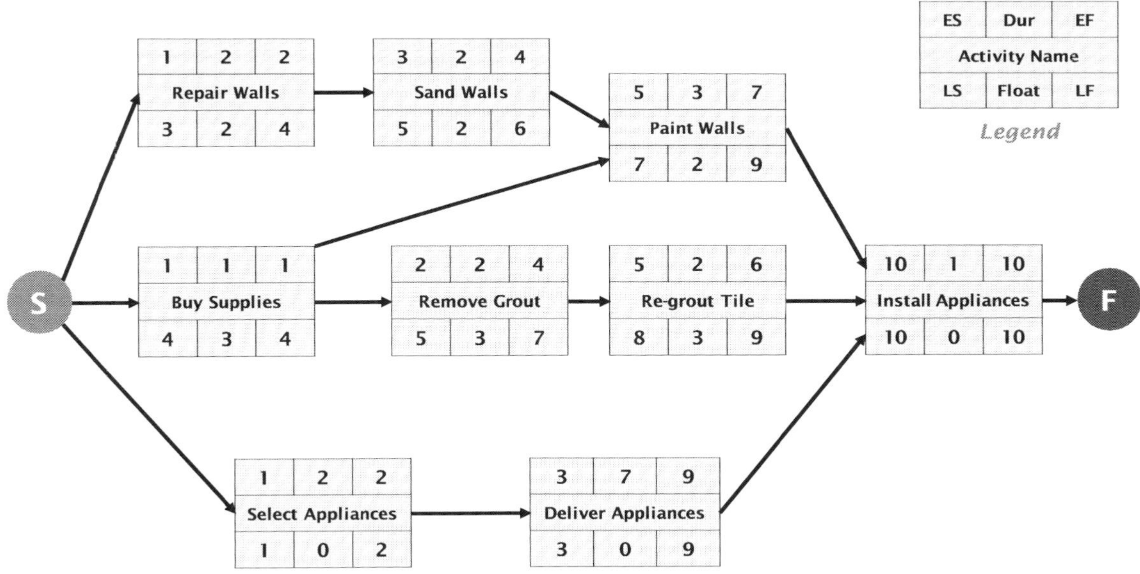

Figure 5-8: Sample Network Logic Diagram

Sequencing for larger, more complex projects can be quite challenging and may require the services of a professional scheduler. Such projects may require knowledge of specialized dependencies (finish-to-finish and start-to-start) and the proper use of leads and lags. These topics are beyond the scope of this book.

5.6.3. Prepare Schedule

Preparing a schedule involves establishing reasonable start and finish dates for all planned project activities. *Reasonable* means that resources are highly likely to be available to do the work when and as scheduled.

Preparing a schedule also involves doing at least rudimentary network analysis to determine which activities control project completion. This sequence of activities is called the *critical path* and exists on every project whether it is known or not. The network logic diagram in the previous section also includes the results of critical path analysis.

Schedules are often displayed in the form of a Gantt Charts as illustrated below.

Schedule for Certification Activities

Proposed

No.	Activities	Start	Finish	2-13	2-20	2-27	3-6	3-13	3-20	3-27
5	**Level B candidates**	**02-09-2017**	**05-02-2017**							
5.1	Complete and submit application	02-09-2017	02-27-2017							
5.2	*Review for compliance*	*02-14-2017*	*03-04-2017*							
5.3	Prepare and submit detail report	02-19-2017	03-14-2017							
5.4	*Score competence elements*	*03-01-2017*	*03-24-2017*							
5.5	Schedule exam	03-06-2017	03-29-2017							
5.6	Prep for exam	02-09-2017	03-29-2017							
5.7	Take exam	02-23-2017	04-12-2017							
5.8	Schedule interview	02-09-2017	03-29-2017							
5.9	Get interviewed	02-23-2017	04-12-2017							
5.10	*Notify of decision*	*04-22-2017*	*05-02-2017*							

Figure 5-9: Sample Gantt Chart

5.7. Management Plans

Management plans are narrative documents that describe the project management team's approach to dealing with the challenges that arise in every project. The depth and detail of each management plan should be determined by the project manager based on the needs of the project. For example:

- On smaller, simpler projects, it may be possible to combine the Stakeholder Engagement Management Plan and the Communications Management Plan.
- If a project is being done entirely with internal resources, a Procurement Management Plan would not be needed.

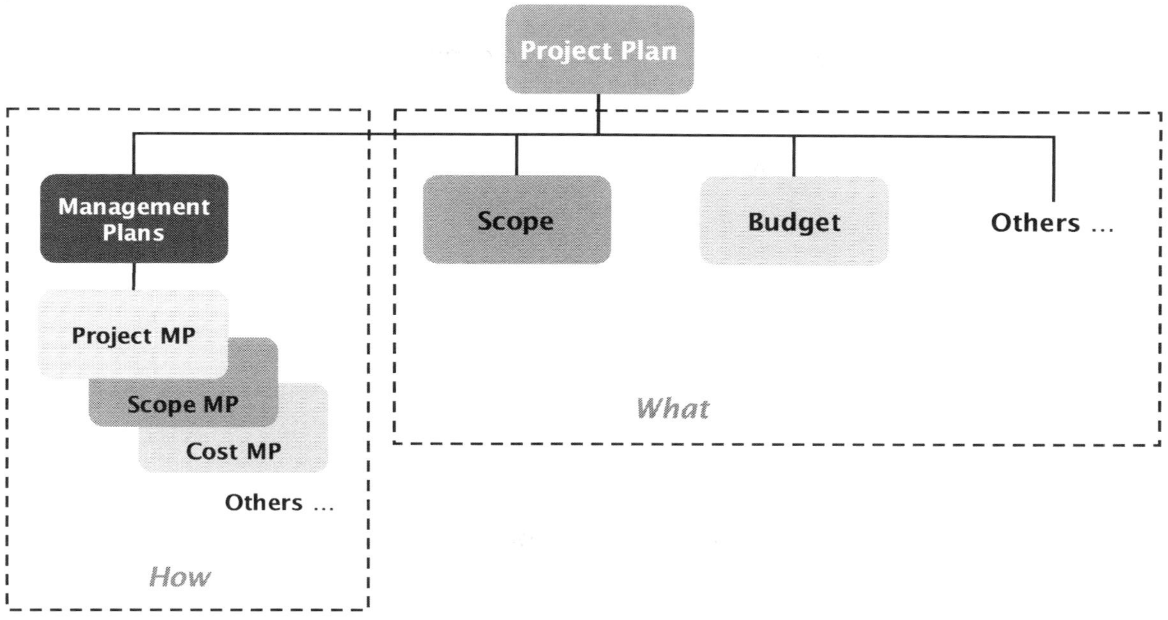

Figure 5-10: Relationship Between the Project Plan and Management Plans

Section 4.3.5 provides more detail about the Sustainability Management Plan. Templates for the other management plans are available from GPM and many other web sources.

Management Plan	Typical Contents
Sustainability Management	▪ Key Performance Indicators (KPIs). These will be as outlined in the P5 Impact Analysis. ▪ Environmental impact assessment. A summary of the planned environmental impact and steps that will be taken to decrease the effects or increase the opportunities identified. ▪ Scope exclusions. Any known areas of potential sustainability impact that the project will not address. ▪ Sustainability risk management. Any differences from standard practices in the approach to identifying, analyzing, and responding to sustainability risks. ▪ Reviews and reporting. Steps to take in a project audit regarding sustainability and how sustainability metrics will be reported throughout the project.
Benefits Realization Management	▪ Roles and responsibilities ▪ Expected benefits and dis-benefits ▪ Benefits measurement process ▪ Reporting
Communications Management	▪ What information each stakeholder needs ▪ Where the information will be found and how it will be accessed and collected ▪ What each report will contain ▪ How the information will be stored ▪ How frequently each report will be distributed ▪ Which stakeholders will get which reports

Management Plan	Typical Contents
Cost Management	▪ Roles and responsibilities ▪ Estimating approach and guidelines ▪ Budgeting approach and guidelines ▪ Units (usually staff hours or currency) ▪ How changes will be managed
Procurement Management	▪ The overall procurement strategy: make or buy, supplier selection practices, etc. ▪ Key products to be purchased, from whom ▪ Acceptance criteria and relevant quality assurance requirements ▪ Methods used to evaluate, select, and manage suppliers ▪ Contractual terms and conditions ▪ Types of pricing and methods of reimbursement ▪ Methods to be used to satisfy legal and regulatory requirements which apply to purchased goods
Quality Management	▪ Objectives ▪ Roles and responsibilities ▪ Processes and methods ▪ Quality practices ▪ Resources ▪ Sequence of quality management activities ▪ Links to organizational quality management processes and systems
Risk Management	▪ General approach ▪ Roles and responsibilities ▪ Budgets and timing ▪ Prioritization approach
Schedule Management	▪ Roles and responsibilities ▪ Scheduling approach and guidelines ▪ Source of scheduling inputs (e.g., Work Breakdown Structure, Master Formats, contract) ▪ How changes will be managed
Scope Management	▪ Roles and responsibilities ▪ General approach ▪ How changes will be managed ▪ How changes will be integrated into the project ▪ Expected stability of scope
Stakeholder Engagement Management	▪ Roles and responsibilities ▪ Stakeholder list ▪ Engagement strategy ▪ Link to communications management plan

Table 5-4: Overview of Contents of Common Management Plans

5.8. Summary

This chapter has detailed the activities involved in managing a PRiSM project lifecycle phase: these activities repeat within each phase. It covers basic concepts for planning, accomplishing, and controlling the work of each phase. The chapter concludes by describing key management plans used to provide oversight and control when using PRiSM.

6. Supporting Processes

6.1. Stakeholder Engagement

Stakeholders are individuals and organizations who can help or harm the project. Their likelihood of helping or harming is based on how the project affects their interests. *Stakeholder engagement* can be regarded as management of social risks and opportunities and should consider both external and internal stakeholders. In a PRiSM project, stakeholders are invited to participate and are *engaged* rather than *managed* to reflect the fact that that most stakeholder relationships involve influence and negotiation rather than control.

Typical project stakeholders are shown in the figure below:

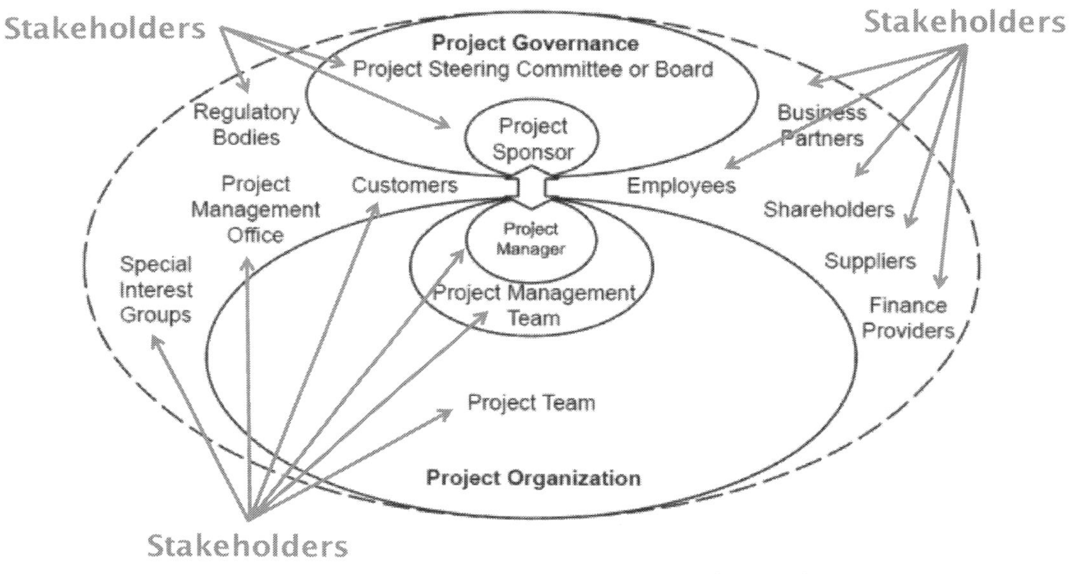

Figure 6-1: Typical Project Stakeholders

Stakeholder engagement should be managed within the project through the project management processes.

Stakeholders will normally include at least the following:

- **Project sponsor** — authorizes the project, makes executive decisions, and solves problems and conflicts beyond the project manager's authority. This role may also be called the *project owner* or *project executive*. Regardless of the name used for the role, this individual and the project manager must agree about the responsibilities of both roles.
- **Project manager** — leads and manages project activities and is accountable for project completion and closure. If the project is terminated early, the project manager remains responsible for closure activities.

- **Project management team** — supports the project manager in leading and managing the project activities.
- **Project team** — performs project activities.

Other stakeholders may include:

- **Project steering committee or board** — contributes to the project by providing senior level guidance.
- **Customers or customer representatives** — contribute by specifying project requirements and accepting the project deliverables.
- **Suppliers** — contribute by supplying resources to the project.
- **Project management office** — performs a wide variety of activities, some of which include governance, standardization, competence development, project planning support, resource allocation, and project monitoring.

6.1.1. Stakeholder Analysis

The *stakeholder analysis* process involves identifying the stakeholders and gathering information on their interest (needs, aims) and power (influence) on the project.

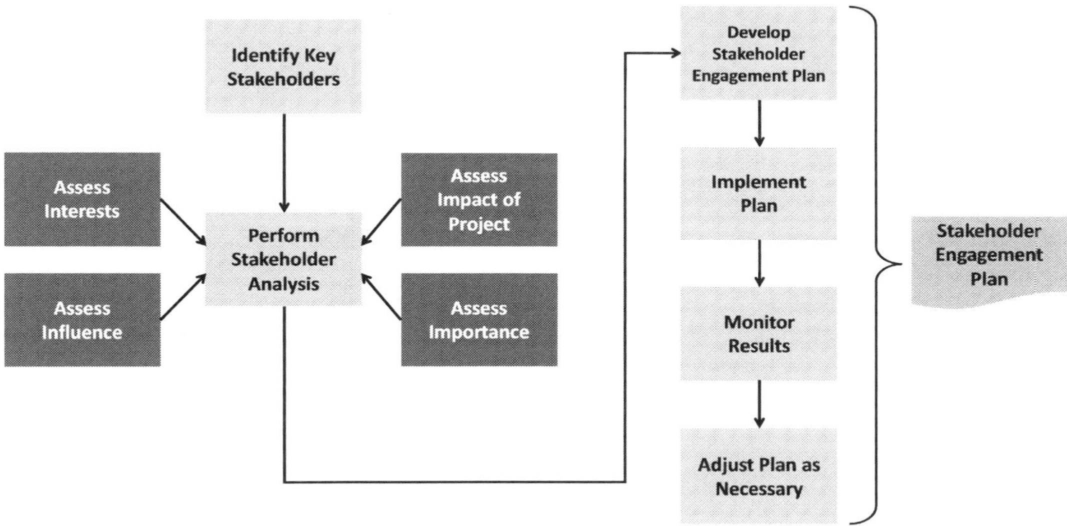

Figure 6-2: Stakeholder Analysis Process

Action plans are developed and implemented to deal with each stakeholder or stakeholder group appropriately. These are monitored and controlled to ensure effectiveness.

The composition and influences of project stakeholders usually change as the project progresses, and often change significantly at phase boundaries. The process of stakeholder analysis is, therefore, applied continuously.

6.1.2. Stakeholder Analysis Matrix

Stakeholder analysis activities establish the individuals and groups with an interest in the project, and prioritize their relative importance in terms of needs and degree of influence on project decisions and activities.

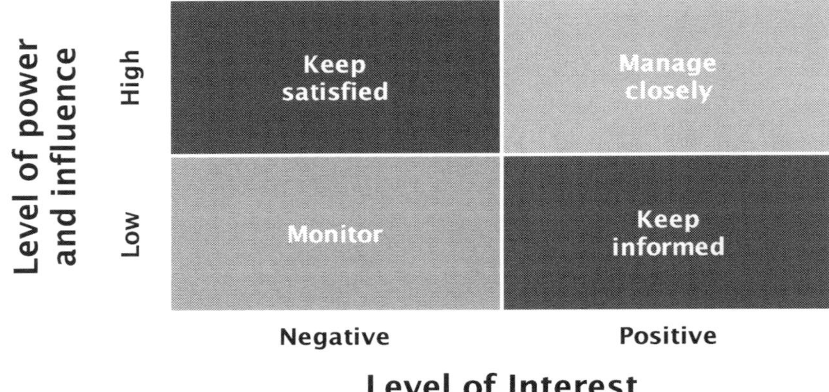

Figure 6-3: Stakeholder Analysis Matrix

The figure above displays one approach to managing stakeholder engagement by classifying stakeholders according to their interest and influence:

- **High Power-High Interest Stakeholders.** These are identified in the upper right block. These people are key to your success, and are not necessarily high ranking executives on your management team. These stakeholders should be fully engaged in external and internal rollout planning and decisions.
- **High Power-Low Interest Stakeholders.** Represented in the top left hand quadrant on the stakeholders chart, these people need less information and less involvement than the high interest stakeholders. But, because they do have power within the organization—formal or informal—to impact the change, it is important to keep them connected and satisfied on progress, but not to overwhelm them with details.
- **Low Power-High Interest Stakeholders.** Represented on the lower right hand quadrant, these are individuals that may have great knowledge of the company but have low influence on organizational change. It is important to keep them well informed so that you can get their valuable feedback. They can help you solve problems when they arise or guide you on how to avoid them in the first place. Keep them informed.
- **Low Power-Low Interest Stakeholders.** In the lower left quadrant are the members of the organization that need only minimum information. The key here is that you are able to make the right determination of who is in this quadrant and that what defines minimal information

6.2. Estimating

As noted earlier, an *estimate* is an informed assessment of an uncertain event. *Informed* means that you have an identified basis for the estimate. *Uncertain* recognizes that multiple outcomes are possible. Estimates are expressed as ranges with each value in the range having a discrete probability of occurrence. Table 6-1 below illustrates some ranges in use for different kinds of projects.

<table>
<tr><th>ANSI Z94.0</th><th>AACEI (US)</th><th>ACostE (UK)</th><th>NASA</th></tr>
<tr><td>Order of Magnitude
(-30/+50)</td><td>Class 5
(-100/+200)</td><td>Order of Magnitude
(-30/+30)</td><td>Level 4
(-45/+45)</td></tr>
<tr><td rowspan="2">Budget
(-15/+30)</td><td>Class 4
(-60/+120)</td><td>Study
(-20/+20)</td><td>Level 5
(-35/+35)</td></tr>
<tr><td>Class 3
(-30/+50)</td><td>Budget
(-10/+10)</td><td>Level 6
(-25/+25)</td></tr>
<tr><td rowspan="2">Definitive
(-5/+15)</td><td>Class 2
(-15/+30)</td><td rowspan="2">Definitive
(-5/+5)</td><td>Level 7
(-15/+15)</td></tr>
<tr><td>Class 1
(-5/+10)</td><td>Level 8
(-5/+5)</td></tr>
</table>

Table 6-1: Comparative Accuracy of Various Estimate Classes

Estimating accuracy should improve (the range of the estimates should decrease) as the project moves through the phases of the PRiSM project lifecycle as more information becomes available.

Most projects will require estimates for effort (staff time), cost, duration, elapsed time, and expected future performance.

Estimates can be made at any level of size or detail. Smaller items and more detailed items will normally have smaller ranges.

6.2.1. The Relationship Between Estimates and Budgets

Again, as noted earlier, a *budget* is a management control and is thus defined as a single number. For example, if we estimate the effort required to complete a design activity as being between 50 and 80 hours of effort with all of the numbers within that range having an equal probability of occurrence, we can take:

- A *conservative* approach, and budget the activity for 80 hours with the expectation that it will almost certainly be completed for *less* than the budget.
- An *aggressive* approach, and budget the activity for 50 hours with the expectation that it will almost certainly be completed for *more* than the budget.
- A *moderate* approach, and budget the activity for 65 hours and expect that it is as likely to be over budget as under budget.

With PRiSM, we will generally take a moderate approach based on the assumption that underruns and overruns will balance out over the course of the entire project.

6.2.2. Estimating Approaches

There are three basic *estimating approaches*:

- **Parametric** — use measurable attributes (square feet of space, lines-of-code, weight of satellite, etc.) in a mathematical model.
- **Analogous** — factor the actual cost of previous, similar projects.
- **Bottom-up** — sum individual item estimates (tasks, activities, work packages).

6.2.3. Basis of Estimate

The *Basis of Estimate* (BOE) is documentation of how the estimate was developed. It details the premise, or basis, for how the estimates were developed. It includes documentation of assumptions, of any studies or analysis used as a reference, and any other details which influenced the estimates.

6.2.4. Three-point Estimates

The most common approach to estimating on projects today is to use *three-point estimates* to describe the range of possible actuals:

- **Most likely** — the value that is more probable than any other.
- **Optimistic** — the lowest reasonable value
- **Pessimistic** — the highest reasonable value

Three-point estimates can be used with any of the basic estimating approaches described above.

Triangular Distribution

Using a *triangular distribution* means that we assume the three-point estimate defines a "curve" in the shape of a triangle. The expected value or mean of the distribution is normally used as the budget for the item estimated and is calculated as follows:

Expected Value = (Optimistic + Most Likely + Pessimistic) ÷ 3

For example, if we think an activity is most likely to take 5 days, unlikely to take less than 4, and equally unlikely to take more than 12, the expected duration would be:

Expected Value = (4 + 5 + 12) = 21 ÷ 3 = 7 days

Program Evaluation and Review Technique (PERT)

Although PERT was originally designed to be used with expected completion dates, on modern projects, it is often used with effort and cost figures as well. When using PERT, the expected value or mean of the distribution is normally used as the budget for the item estimated. This is calculated as follows:

Expected Value = (Optimistic + (4 x Most Likely) + Pessimistic) ÷ 6

For example, if we think an activity is most likely to take 5 days, unlikely to take less than 4, and equally unlikely to take more than 12, the expected duration with PERT would be:

Expected Value = (4 + (4 x 5) + 12) = 36 ÷ 6 = 6 days

6.2.5. Summing Estimates

Since estimates are ranges, statistical techniques must be used to sum them. Cost and effort estimates can be summed using the Method of Moments. Cost, effort, and duration estimates can be summed using a Monte Carlo simulation. Both approaches require a minimum of 25 data points (estimates) for their results to be reliable.

Remember that the results of these calculations are still estimates: because of the uncertainty of the inputs, there is uncertainty in the outputs as well.

Method of Moments

Calculate the expected value of each distribution as described above. Total the expected values to obtain the expected value for the project.

Calculate the variance of each distribution using the following formulas:

Triangular Distribution = $((\text{Pessimistic} - \text{Optimistic}) \div 5)^2$

PERT = $((\text{Pessimistic} - \text{Optimistic}) \div 6)^2$

Sum the variances, then take the square root of that number to obtain the standard deviation for the project. Use one of the following approximations for an estimate of the project range:

±1 standard deviation = 70% likelihood of results within that range
±2 standard deviations = 90% likelihood of results within that range
±3 standard deviations = 99% likelihood of results within that range

Monte Carlo Simulation

To perform a Monte Carlo simulation, use a random number generator to select a random value from within the range of each estimate. Add these numbers to obtain the results for the first trial. Run additional trials (usually at least 100, although simulations with 1000 trials are not uncommon) and record the results. Calculate the expected value (mean) and the standard deviation of the trial results. Use the approximations above for an estimate of the project range.

6.3. Team Development

Team development is fundamentally about trying to create a situation where "the whole is greater than the sum of the parts."

6.3.1. Teams vs. Work Groups

Teams are based on mutual accountability rather than individual accountability. An effective team is cohesive, aware of the success criteria, motivated towards achieving them, and committed to supporting other team members. Typically, team members communicate well, share information, and make decisions together.

6.3.2. Team Building Activities

Team building activities can be used to enhance team performance through:

- Building more effective working relationships
- Reducing team members' role ambiguity
- Finding solutions to team problems

Fun is an important component to team building, but the project manager must remember that the intended result is to become more productive, more focused, and better aligned. Team building activities should be chosen to suit the team's personalities or the results may be damaging rather than constructive.

6.3.3. Tuckman's Stages of Team Development

Figure 6-4: Tuckman's Stages of Team Development

In 1965, Dr. Bruce W. Tuckman suggested that teams need to go through three stages of development before reaching the fourth stage of *performing*:

- **Forming** — the team is established. Individuals are anxious about their personal identity, role, the impression they make, and the attitudes and backgrounds of others.
- **Storming** — differences emerge between individuals as they sort out their roles. This stage is characterized by hostility and disruption.
- **Norming** — the team develops ways of working together. Closer relationships are created and real camaraderie may emerge. Roles and norms are established.
- **Performing** — the team becomes productive.

In Figure 6-4 above, the black text describes what the team members are doing at each stage while the green text describes how they are usually feeling. The project manager's behavior will also vary by stage with the project manager generally being more relationship-oriented in the first three stages and more task-oriented in the final one.

Project managers need to understand these stages (and feelings) to help their teams reach the performing stage. For example, attempts to avoid storming can actually prevent the team from moving forward.

6.4. Performance Monitoring and Control

Performance monitoring (also called *status reporting, progress reporting*, or *performance measurement*) is the process of collecting and reporting information about how the project is progressing towards its objective. The purpose of performance monitoring is to discover variations from plan.

Control is the process of analyzing that information, evaluating the impact of variations, and responding as necessary. The purpose of control is to determine the best way to achieve the project's success criteria. Tolerances and triggers allow work to continue when the variations are minor.

In general, project performance should be checked at least monthly, and more often if the project scope is unstable or the project is expected to take less than a year.

6.4.1. Performance Measures

Virtually all projects should report performance against the following measures:

- **Planned costs** — amounts expected to be spent. These amount may also be called *budgeted costs*, and if they have been assigned to a particular time period, *scheduled costs*.
- **Actual costs** — amounts spent on project activities. Actual costs include labor, materials, rentals, and purchases. Actual costs are usually reported in monetary units (dollars, euros, yuan, etc.), but they may also be reported in labor hours.
- **Work completed** — this may involve a simple count of completed activities or more complex measures as described below in Section 6.4.3 on Earned Value Management.
- **Schedule results** — a comparison of planned start and finish dates to actual start and finish dates.
- **Stakeholder satisfaction** — are the key stakeholders satisfied with the project to-date?

Many projects, particularly larger projects and projects using contractors to do much of the work, will also want to report performance against the following measures:

- **Committed costs** — amounts that have been set aside for future work.
- **Accrued costs** — amounts owed for work that has been done but not yet recorded as an actual.
- **Cashflow** — the difference between amounts paid and amounts received.

6.4.2. Variance Analysis

Variance analysis involves comparing the current (actual) state of the project to its expected (planned) state. Both the current state and the expected state can be measured used any of the performance measures described above. Variance analysis can compare static data or trends (also called *trend analysis*).

Variance analysis is used to provide guidance for taking corrective action by forecasting future performance. In preparing and using such forecasts, project managers should keep in mind the insight from statistician Charles Box: all forecasts are lies; some forecasts are useful.

Earned Value Management, described in Section 6.4.3 below, is fundamentally a form of variance analysis.

Variance analysis typically includes tolerances and triggers for each measure as illustrated in the figure above. Tolerances and triggers should be defined for each of the project's success criteria to facilitate decision-making at the appropriate management level. For example, variances within the tolerance limits for a given work package would be handled by the manager at that level without involvement from the sponsor or project manager.

<table>
<tr><th rowspan="2">% of Budget</th><th colspan="2">Typical Management Response</th><th rowspan="2">Red/ Amber/ Green</th></tr>
<tr><th>Activity Results</th><th>Cumulative Results</th></tr>
<tr><td>+20 or more</td><td rowspan="3">Investigate</td><td rowspan="2">Corrective Action</td><td rowspan="2">Red</td></tr>
<tr><td>+15</td></tr>
<tr><td>+10</td><td>Investigate</td><td>Amber</td></tr>
<tr><td>+5</td><td rowspan="3">No action</td><td rowspan="4">No action</td><td rowspan="4">Green</td></tr>
<tr><td>0</td></tr>
<tr><td>-5</td></tr>
<tr><td>-10</td><td rowspan="3">Investigate</td></tr>
<tr><td>-15</td><td>Investigate</td><td rowspan="2">Amber</td></tr>
<tr><td>-20 or more</td><td>Corrective Action</td></tr>
</table>

Figure 6-5: Typical Management Response to Variances

Tolerances are often defined through a color coding system: Red-Amber-Green (RAG) after the colors of traffic lights.

6.4.3. Earned Value Management

Earned value management (EVM) compares the amount of completed work to the amount of planned work at any time in the project. To be effective, earned value measurements must be applied and analyzed at both project and detail levels. Variances show areas that are under- or over-achieving.

Earned value management uses the following measures:

- **Planned Value (PV)** — the amount budgeted for each activity or deliverable sorted by the reporting period when it is expected to be spent. PV includes all of the work of the project.
- **Actual Cost (AC)** — the amounts spent for the work accomplished.
- **Earned Value (EV)** — the amounts budgeted for the work accomplished.

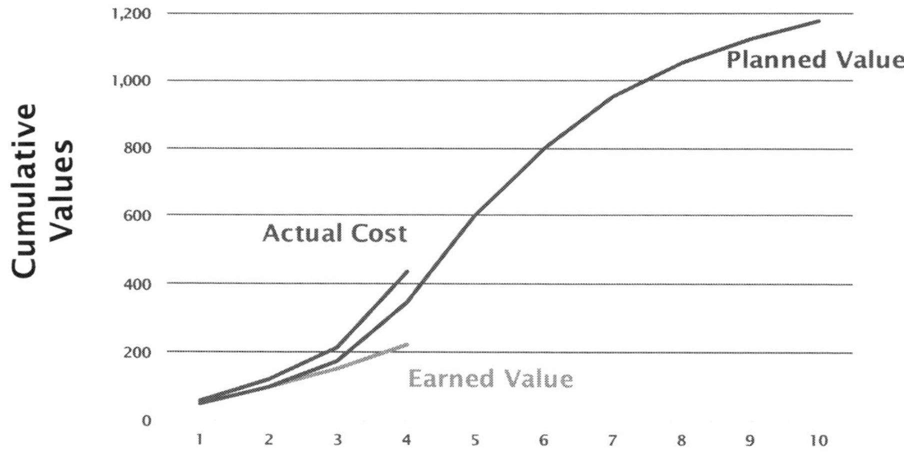

Figure 6-6: Earned Value Measures

Following is a simple example based on the chart above. This project has:

- A total budget of $1.2 million
- 1,000 activities with an expected cost of $1,200 each
- A 10-month schedule

Planned value is established first. Each of the activities has been assigned to a specific month based on a schedule that was prepared using critical path analysis. As well, the schedule has been analyzed for resource usage and the necessary resources have been committed. Since the number of staff assigned to the project will start out slow, then ramp up in the middle of the project before tapering off at the end, the Planned Value line shows the classic "s-curve" shape.

After four months, 175 activities have been completed at a total cost of $420,000. The schedule called for 320 activities to be complete at the end of month 4 at a cost of $384,000. We can use this information to calculate the variances shown in the table below.

Metric	Formula	Sample Values
Planned Value	Input	384,000
Actual Cost		420,000
Earned Value		210,000
Cost Variance	EV – AC	-210,000
Schedule Variance	EV – PV	-174,000
Cost Performance Index	EV ÷ AC	0.50
Schedule Performance Index	EV ÷ PV	0.55

Table 6-2: Sample Earned Value Formulas

The performance indices can be used to predict future project performance. For example, if we assume that project performance to-date is representative of likely future performance, we can divide the total project budget by the CPI to get a prediction that our project will cost $2.4 million before it's done.

6.4.4. Corrective Action

Corrective action is anything done to improve the project's chances of meeting its success criteria. It is typically taken in response to variances from plan, but it can also be taken in response to changes in the outside environment, and in particular, in response to changes that affect the business case.

The most extreme form of corrective action is cancelling the project.

Corrective action normally involves adding, deleting, or modifying activities. Any such changes should be handled through the change control process.

6.5. Change Control

The purpose of *change control* is to ensure traceability and accountability for any modifications made to project documentation such as the project plan or product descriptions. Uncontrolled changes will undermine the validity of baseline plans and forecasts. Uncontrolled change is a frequent cause of project failure.

Any changes should be clearly and swiftly communicated to the relevant stakeholders to ensure that there is no misunderstanding of what versions or what specifications the project is working to.

Note that change control practices should *never* be used to stifle change. Change is normal and natural on all projects. Changes may be generated internally by the project team or externally by clients, regulators, or the needs of the funding organization.

6.5.1. Change Control Board

A *change control board* (CCB), also called a change advisory board, has ultimate responsibility for approving changes. On smaller, less complex projects, the CCB may be the project sponsor or the project manager. On larger, more complex projects, it will typically include other key stakeholders as well. When the project has a steering committee or project board, that entity will often function as the CCB.

On very large or very complex projects, there can be multiple CCBs with responsibility for different kinds of changes. In every case, responsibilities must be clearly defined.

6.5.2. Change Control Process

A typical change control process is shown in Figure 6-7 below:

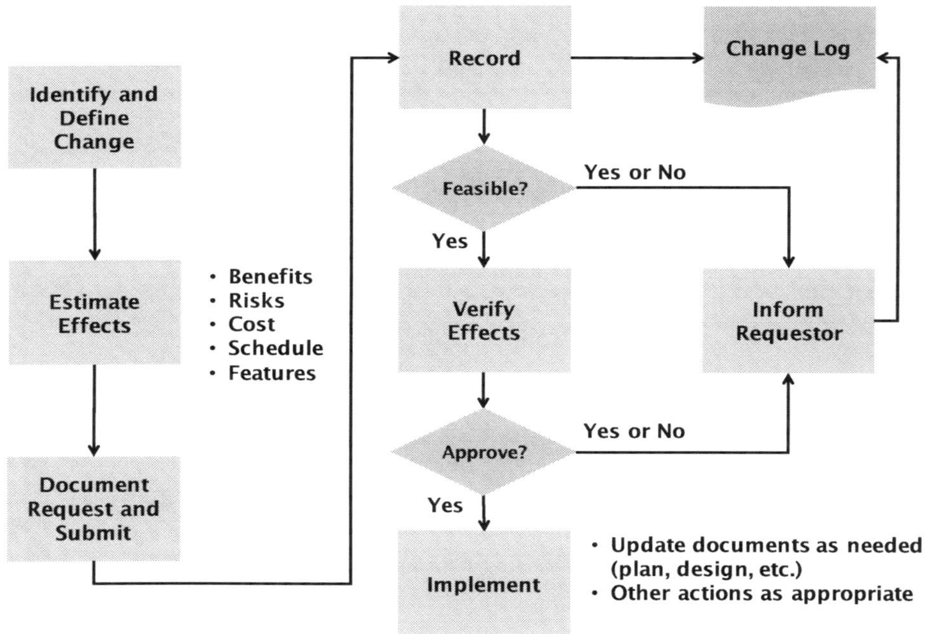

Figure 6-7: Change Control Process Flowchart

Requests may come from any stakeholder. All requests should be made on a change request form and recorded in a change request register (change request log).

The change request process should capture the following information:

- **Description** — a narrative description of the change along with the date submitted, the priority, the reason for the change, and expected benefits.
- **Impact assessment** — how will the disposition of the change (accepted or rejected) affect the project? The change should be evaluated against at least the Business Case and the P5 factors. Assessment includes estimating cost, schedule, risk, and quality impacts.
- **Disposition** — was the change accepted, rejected, or modified?
- **Updates** — what documentation was modified as a result of the disposition?

6.6. Configuration Management

The purpose of *configuration management* is to ensure the integrity of the deliverables by ensuring that their description (specification) matches their actual form and function. It is most commonly applied to physical products but can be applied to documents such as the project plan as well.

The configuration of an item defines what it is (observable characteristics) and what it does (functional characteristics). A configuration item is a product or component controlled by the configuration management system. A configuration item can only be changed through the change control process.

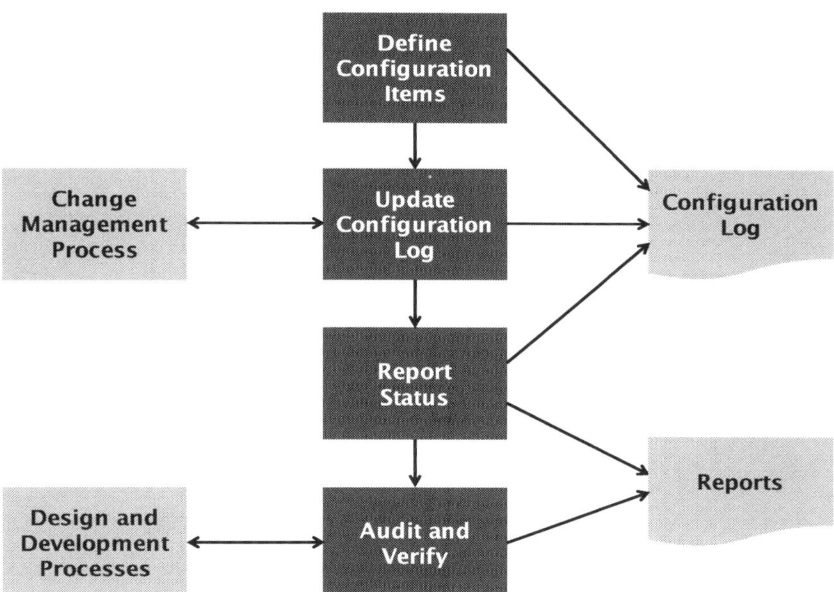

Figure 6-8: Configuration Management Process Flowchart

Configuration management is undertaken alongside the change control process and involves four main activities: identification, control, status accounting, and auditing:

- **Identification** — products that are to be controlled are called configuration items. The items to be controlled are identified by the project team and approved by the project manager. Each item is given a unique reference number.

- **Control** — once a configuration item comes under control, it is "frozen." This means that the change process must be applied before the configuration (description) of the item can be changed. This prevents ad hoc changes and ensures that changes can be tracked during the life of the configuration item.
- **Status accounting** — all approved changes are recorded in a log (register).
- **Auditing** — checks are made to ensure that each item conforms to its technical specification and that each component in a system is compatible with others.

6.7. Sustainable Procurement

Procurement is the process of obtaining products or services from outside the performing organization. It is also called contacting, acquisition, or tendering. It covers financial appraisal of the options available, development of a procurement strategy, selection of suppliers, preparation of contract documentation, and management of the agreed contracts. The procurement process is illustrated in the diagram below.

For a project to be sustainable, any procurement activities must also be sustainable. This generally requires including:

- Sustainability considerations as part of procurement planning.
- Past social and environmental performance of potential suppliers among the criteria for supplier selection.
- Social and environmental performance during the project as a factor in supplier reviews.

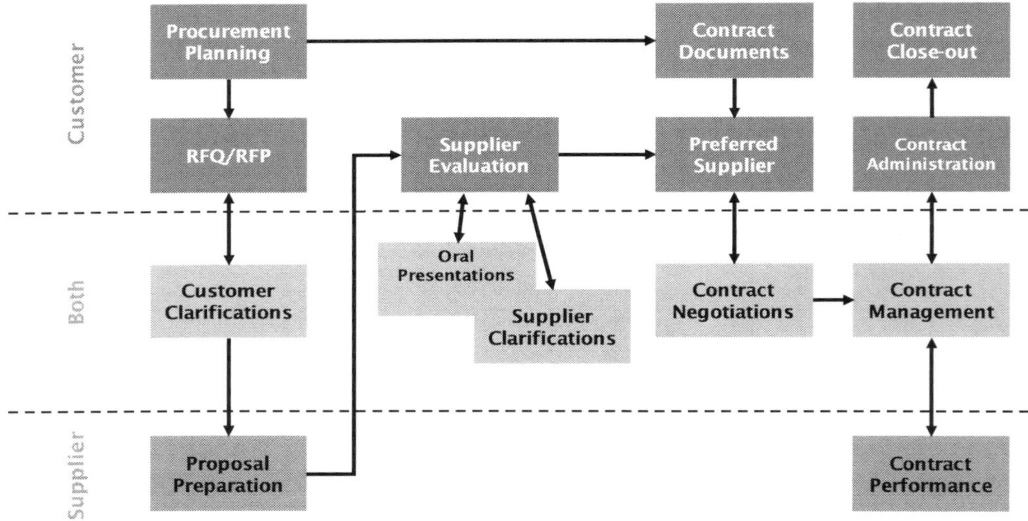

Figure 6-9: Procurement Process

6.7.1. Procurement Planning

Unless the project will be done without any procurement (i.e., done entirely with internal resources), the project management team should prepare a Procurement Management Plan as described in Section 5.7. The plan should reflect any relevant organizational policies and procedures.

6.7.2. Request for Proposal

A *request for proposal* (RFP) is a document prepared by the customer which describes what the customer would like to purchase and how it plans to manage the contract. It may also be called a request for quotation (RFQ) or an invitation to bid (ITB). An RFP will normally include all of the following items:

- Introduction or overview
- Statement of Work (SOW)
- Decision process and schedule
- Format of the response
- Contract type
- Contact person
- Required contract terms

The SOW is a narrative description of what the supplier is expected to deliver. It should include:

- Characteristics of the item to be supplied
- Schedule requirements
- Cost requirements
- Reporting requirements
- P5 compliance requirements

6.7.3. Contract Type

There are five major contract types:

- Fixed price (also called lump sum)
- Unit price (also called re-measurable)
- Cost reimbursable (also called cost plus)
- Incentive fee
- Hybrid

The table below illustrates the key characteristics of each type.

Contract Type	Amount Paid to Supplier	Cost Risk Borne by
Fixed Price	One total amount as specified in the contract; usually paid in increments	Supplier
Unit Price	Fixed price by line item with quantities allowed to vary with limits	Supplier
Cost Reimbursable	Based on supplier's actual costs	Mostly by customer
Incentive fee	Fixed price or cost reimbursable as agreed with incentives or penalties as agreed	Shared
Hybrid	A combination of the above	Varies by item

Table 6-3: Characteristics of Major Contract Types

A fixed price contract means that the supplier will bear any losses from price increases in return for obtaining the benefits of price decreases. Fixed price does not directly affect either technical or schedule risk, although the supplier may be tempted to compromise quality to reduce the impact of overruns. Fixed price contracts typically require a more detailed description of the item to be purchased in order to allow the supplier to make an informed decision about accepting the cost risk. Any change to the product characteristics requires an adjustment to the price.

A unit price contract requires a list of items or components with unit prices for each. For example, on a highway construction project, units might include labor, equipment use, gravel, and concrete with estimated quantities of each. Suppliers agree to deliver items for the unit price, and quantities are allowed to vary within specified limits without triggering a price adjustment.

A cost reimbursable contract requires visibility into the supplier's actual costs including fringe benefits for employees and overhead amounts such as rent and general management. With cost reimbursable contracts, changes to product characteristics are usually easier to make since the supplier cannot lose money. Many cost reimbursable contracts include incentives to encourage the supplier to exercise good management control.

The type of contract should be selected based on the needs of the project. For example, fixed price contracts usually work best for products with well-defined requirements. Cost reimbursable contracts are better when the requirements are uncertain.

6.7.4. Supplier Identification

Most larger organizations will maintain a database of suppliers who have been pre-qualified for certain types of work. When such a database is available, the RFP should be sent to qualified businesses.

If there is no database, the project management team will have to develop its own list of potential suppliers. This can be done by researching business directories, industrial libraries, and trade journals, or through networking.

Potential suppliers may also be identified by advertising in professional journals and local publications.

In situations where it is known for certain that only a few suppliers have the necessary abilities, the project management team may identify those suppliers directly: this is called *short-listing*. Whenever possible, a short-list should include at least three potential suppliers.

In extreme cases, or when time is of the essence, the procurement may be limited to a single potential supplier: this is called *sole source* procurement.

6.7.5. Selection Criteria and Weights

Selection criteria and *weights* (the relative importance of the selection criteria) should be driven by the likely effect on the project success criteria and on the sustainability factors. Selection criteria for a PRiSM project should always include the P5 costs and benefits caused by the potential supplier and its supply chain.

Other criteria will depend on the nature of the item being purchased.

6.7.6. Supplier Selection

There are two major approaches to supplier selection:

- **Lowest price, technically acceptable.** Prospective suppliers submit technical and commercial (cost) proposals separately. The technical proposals are screened or scored against the defined selection criteria. Commercial proposals for all technically compliant suppliers are then opened, and the lowest price is selected.
- **Best value.** Proposals are still scored against defined criteria, but with this approach, cost is just another criterion. The highest score is selected.

The key in both cases is to define appropriate criteria, and to evaluate those criteria as objectively as possible.

Once a supplier has been selected, it will be necessary to negotiate and sign a contract. Some contracts are simple and straightforward; others are not. For example, a personal services contract for a technical expert might only require 4-5 pages while a contract for highway construction could easily require a few hundred pages.

6.7.7. Contract Management

Once the contract is in place, it must be managed. The focus of contract management is to ensure that both parties adhere to the stated terms and conditions.

6.7.8. Contract Close-out

Once the work of the contract has been completed, it must be closed-out. This normally includes:

- Verification that the supplier has accomplished all administrative tasks. These may include return of the customer's property, disposition of classified or confidential material, and settlement of any sub-contracts.
- Settlement of outstanding issues such as disallowed costs or un-liquidated advances.
- Verification that the work is actually complete and that no overpayments have been made.
- Release of any unneeded amounts from the organization's budgeting system.
- Ensuring that all required paperwork has been submitted to the proper authorities.
- Approval of the final payment.
- Obtaining a contract completion statement from the supplier.
- Disposition of files

Some of the information in the contract files must be kept for a specific number of years. These record-keeping retention requirements are sometimes the result of external legal requirement, and sometimes included in the contract's terms and conditions.

6.8. Issue Management

In PRiSM, an *issue* is defined as a realized risk or opportunity that cannot be handled by the project manager. This is often because the project manager lacks either the authority or the resources to deal with the issue. Issues differ from problems in that problems can be resolved by the project manager.

Issues that remain unresolved are likely to interfere with the project's success criteria and may even cause outright project failure.

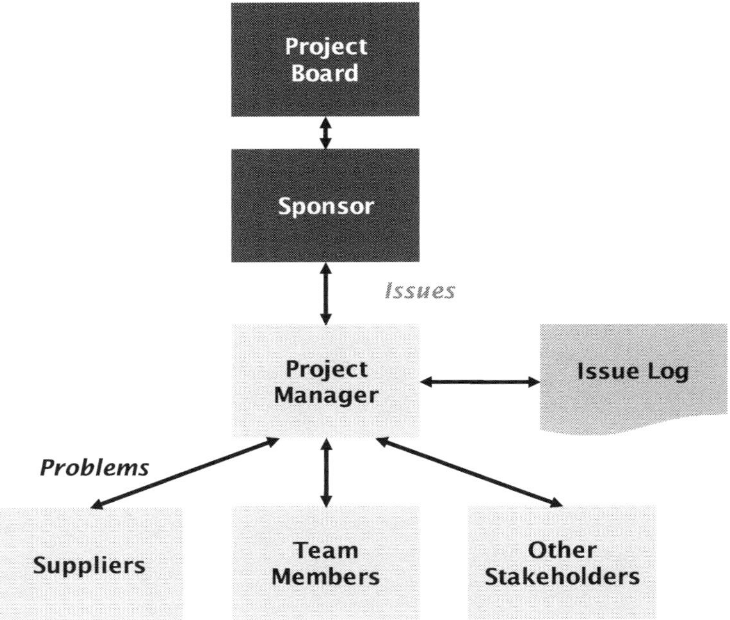

Figure 6-10: Issue Management Process Relationships

The diagram above illustrates a typical issue management process. Identified issues are recorded in an issue log which can then be used to monitor issue status. All issues are escalated to the project sponsor for resolution. Open issues are reviewed during project status review meetings.

Common challenges in issue management include:

- Failing to escalate issues in a timely manner.
- Diverting the sponsor by escalating problems.

6.9. Summary

This chapter has provided an overview of the processes that support PRiSM. These processes, are: stakeholder engagement, estimating, team development, performance monitoring and control, change control, configuration management, and issues management. Each process itself is used throughout the PRiSM lifecycle and helps to ensure that the project is on track to deliver the outcomes and benefits expected by stakeholders.

Notes

PART THREE: Getting More from PRiSM

Notes

7. Governance

7.1. What is Governance?

Governance is the establishment of rules and practices by which management ensures accountability, fairness, responsiveness, and transparency in the organization's relationships with its stakeholders. Governance can be subtle and may not be easily observable. Governance is about the culture and environment in which the organization and its stakeholders interact. Governance includes:

- Explicit agreements between the organization and its stakeholders for distribution of responsibilities, rights, and rewards.
- Explicit agreements between the organization and its stakeholders about who participates in activities and decisions and to what extent.
- Procedures for reconciling the sometimes conflicting interests of stakeholders in accordance with their duties, privileges, and roles.
- Procedures for proper supervision, control, and information flows to serve as a system of checks and balances.

Good governance is about the rules and practices for making and implementing decisions. It's not as much about making *correct* decisions as it is about defining and following the *best possible process* for making those decisions.

A good decision-making process, and therefore good governance, will have a positive effect on many aspects of the organization including stakeholder engagement policies and practices, meeting procedures, service quality protocols, employee conduct, role definition, and good working relationships. A good decision-making process will also help to ensure that the organization acts prudently, legally, and ethically.

Effective governance encourages organizations to create value through innovation, development, and exploration, and to provide accountability and control systems commensurate with the risks involved.

There are many effective approaches to good governance.

7.1.1. Governance Frameworks

Governance frameworks have been developed to communicate the relationship between different levels of governance in an organization. This is of particular importance in the context of project management where a delineation of responsibility between the company board, the project sponsors, and the project managers is required.

This involves establishing a number of discrete components, namely: organization, corporate governance, governance of project management, and project management. This is illustrated in the figure below.

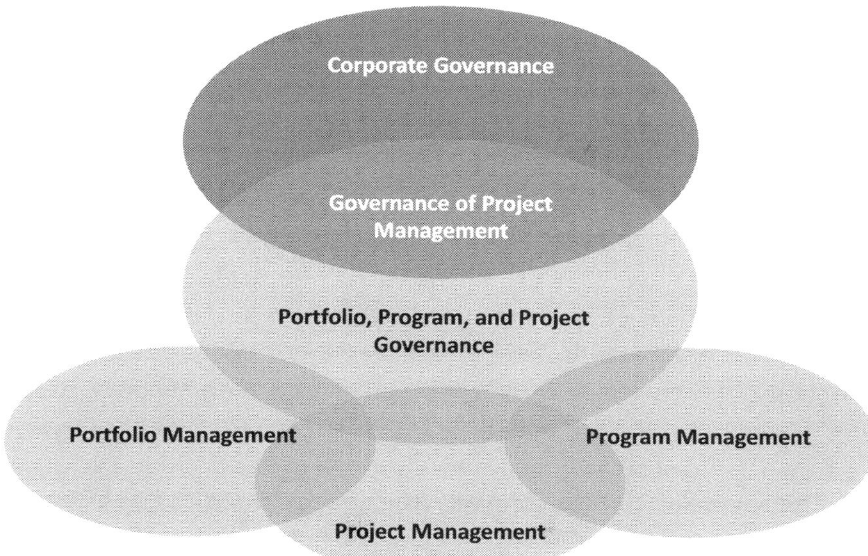

Figure 7-1: Governance Framework for Projects

To clearly identify the different application of governance and to show how corporate governance and project management interface, the term *governance of project management* has been identified. These elements will be discussed later in this section.

When we examine corporate governance in the context of projects, programs, and other change initiatives, it is important to understand the key activities and functions that are undertaken.

Strategic objectives are established by the board of the organization and are communicated through its strategic plan. These objectives and goals are used to identify, select, and prioritize projects and programs as part the organization's portfolio management approach.

Portfolio direction is set by a governance body such as a strategic investment committee and involves establishing the desired portfolio mix and determining appropriate selection criteria and weightings to ensure that a balanced portfolio is achieved.

Sponsorship is a function that exists at the project and program level. It is a role that may be performed by an individual or by a group such as a project steering committee or a program board. The project sponsor is covered in more detail in Section 7.6.2 below. For large or more mature organizations, a specific governance framework may exist to provide oversight for the hundreds or even thousands of projects operating at any given time.

Project management is the function of managing the delivery of a specific project. It is important to understand that project management is not a governance function *per se*. However, there is a governance function that is undertaken by the project manager, and the project manager must operate within the context of project governance. This is dealt with in more detail in Section 7.2.4 below.

Disclosure and reporting is a key principle of governance, and is a practice embedded in project management, governance of project management, and corporate governance. Development of reports not only aids in communication and information dissemination, but reports also capture the status at a given point in time and form part of the corporate record.

The governance framework will be unique for each organization; however, it will conform to a range of key principles. The framework should:

- Promote transparent and fair markets and the efficient allocation of resources.
- Be consistent with the rule of law and support effective supervision and enforcement.
- Protect and facilitate the exercise of shareholder rights and ensure the equitable treatment of all shareholders, including minority and foreign shareholders. All shareholders should have the opportunity to obtain effective redress for violation of their rights.
- Provide sound incentives throughout the investment chain and provide for stock markets to function in a way that contributes to good corporate governance.
- Recognize the rights of stakeholders established by law or through mutual agreements and encourage active co-operation between corporations and stakeholders in creating wealth, jobs, and the sustainability of financially sound enterprises.
- Ensure that timely and accurate disclosure is made on all material matters regarding the corporation, including the financial situation, performance, ownership, and governance of the company.
- Ensure the strategic guidance of the company, the effective monitoring of management by the board, and the board's accountability to the company and the shareholders.

7.1.2. Corporate Governance

Corporate governance involves a set of relationships between a company's management, its board, its shareholders, and other stakeholders. Corporate governance also provides the structure through which the objectives of the company are set, and the means of attaining those objectives and monitoring performance are determined.

Corporate governance occurs at a whole-of-organization level with a major focus on *business as usual* operations. Good corporate governance should provide proper incentives for the board and management to pursue objectives that are in the interests of the company and its shareholders and should facilitate effective monitoring.

Many stock exchanges around the world have specified requirements for listed companies. In the United Kingdom (UK), for example, the UK Corporate Governance Code sets standards of good practice in relation to board leadership and effectiveness, remuneration, accountability, and relations with shareholders. Taking a principle-based approach, the Code sets forth rules for the operation of publicly listed companies.

The Code's principles are intended to help policy makers evaluate and improve the legal, regulatory, and institutional framework for corporate governance with a view to support economic efficiency, sustainable growth, and financial stability. This is primarily achieved by providing shareholders, board members, and executives as well as financial intermediaries and suppliers, with the right incentives to perform their roles within a framework of checks and balances.

The Code's principles recognize the interests of employees and other stakeholders and their important role in contributing to the long-term success and performance of the company. Other factors relevant to a company's decision-making processes, such as environmental anti-corruption or ethical concerns, are considered in the principles but are treated more explicitly in a number of other instruments including the Organization for Economic Cooperation and Development (OECD) *Guidelines for Multinational Enterprises*, OECD's *Convention on Combating Bribery of Foreign Public Officials in International Business Transactions*, the United Nations (UN) *Guiding Principles on Business and Human Rights*, and the International Labor Organization (ILO) *Declaration on Fundamental Principles and Rights at Work*, which are referenced in the principles.

7.2. Levels of Governance Affecting Projects

Governance, as it applies to projects, programs, and portfolios, comprises the value system, responsibilities, processes, and policies that allow projects to achieve organizational activities and foster implementation that is in the best interests of all stakeholders, both internal and external, and the corporation itself.

7.2.1. Portfolio Governance

Portfolio governance is focused on the roles and responsibilities for portfolio management and on ensuring that the appropriate decision-making process and organizational controls are in place and functioning effectively and efficiently. It includes establishment and maintenance of structures, procedures, and methods in order to ensure appropriate governance of projects and programs within the portfolio.

Portfolio governance decisions include:

- Acceptance of projects into the portfolio based upon the organization's strategy, the portfolio optimization strategy, and the organization's capabilities.
- Prioritizing projects, including start, end, suspension, and termination of projects.
- Allocation of resources to projects based on project priorities.
- Identification of skills bottlenecks which risk delays in delivery of projects within the portfolio.
- Possible remedies and mitigation strategies for any risks or issues encountered within the portfolio.

7.2.2. Program Governance

Thiry suggests that program governance consists of developing the program vision and objective while ensuring alignment to the business strategy and stakeholder needs. Effective program governance involves putting in place the right structures and allocating the resources necessary to achieve the vision. Finally, it means putting in place the necessary monitoring and control systems to make the right decisions and realign the program if necessary.

The focus of program governance is efficiency. It is also developing a fit for purpose product requires constant adaptation of project outcomes to changing market needs. In doing so, program governance requires:

- Developing a program vision and objectives
- Putting in place the right structures for decision-making
- Allocating resources to achieve the vision
- Putting in place necessary monitoring and control systems
- Oversight of benefits management
- Ensuring project business cases are sound and in line with the program vision and objectives

7.2.3. Project Management Governance

Governance of project management is a responsibility of corporate management requiring the support of project sponsors, project managers, and project teams. Effective governance of project management will ensure that the organization's projects are aligned to the organization's strategic objectives, and that they are delivered efficiently and sustainably.

Figure 7-1 shows that the activities involved in the governance of project management are a subset of corporate governance. It shows that most project management activities are outside the responsibility of corporate governance. This suggests that the control of projects must be shared between corporate governance and project management.

7.2.4. Project Governance

Project governance is a set of management systems, rules, protocols, relationships, and structures that provide the framework within which decisions are made for project development and implementation to achieve the intended business or strategic motivation (Bekker & Steyn).

ISO 21500:2012 indicates that project governance may include subjects such as defining the management structure; the policies, processes, and methodologies to be used; limits of authority for decision-making; stakeholder responsibilities and accountabilities; and interactions such as reporting and the escalation of issues or risks.

Project governance is specific to the delivery of projects and change within an organization. It is an oversight function that occurs throughout the project lifecycle and typically includes:

- Acceptance criteria for project success and deliverables
- Escalation process
- Organizational charts and defined roles and responsibilities for the project
- Project lifecycle and methodology
- Stage gate or phase reviews

The responsibility for maintaining the appropriate governance of a project is usually assigned to the project sponsor or to a project steering committee (ISO, 2012).

To summarize, project governance:

- Provides a framework for ethical decision-making
- Is based on transparency, accountability, and defined roles
- Sets parameters for management action
- Defines project goals and the means by which they should be achieved

7.3. Characteristics of Good Governance

The following are characteristics of good governance.

- **Participation.** All involved should have a voice in decision-making, either directly or through legitimate intermediate institutions that represent their interests. Such broad participation is built on freedom of association and speech, as well as capacities to participate constructively.
- **Rule of law.** Legal frameworks should be fair and enforced impartially, particularly the laws on human rights.
- **Transparency.** Transparency is built on the free flow of information. Processes, institutions, and information are directly accessible to those concerned with them, and enough information is provided to understand and monitor them.
- **Responsiveness.** Institutions and processes try to serve all stakeholders.
- **Consensus orientation.** Good governance mediates differing interests to reach a broad consensus on what is in the best interests of the group and, where possible, on policies and procedures.
- **Equity.** All men and women have opportunities to improve or maintain their well-being.
- **Effectiveness and efficiency.** Processes and institutions produce results that meet needs while making the best use of resources.
- **Accountability.** Decision makers in government, the private sector, and civil society organizations are accountable to the public, as well as to institutional stakeholders. This accountability differs depending on the organizations and whether the decision is internal or external to an organization.
- **Strategic vision.** Leaders and the public have a broad and long-term perspective on good governance and human development, along with a sense of what is needed for such development. There is also an understanding of the historical, cultural, and social complexities in which that perspective is grounded.

7.4. Why is Project Governance Important?

There are many reasons why projects require governance arrangements. The subsections below explain the major reasons that consistently emerge from research in this area.

7.4.1. Enhance Prospects for Success

True project success is gauged by the realization of business benefits, not only the on-time, on-budget, on-spec delivery of outputs.

Potential for success and value to the business increases when senior business managers actively participate in project governance throughout the project lifecycle. This includes decision making and promoting the organizational change needed to achieve the anticipated business value.

Failure factors such as poor alignment to strategy, inadequate information, unclear requirements, inadequate resourcing, and poor communication are more likely to be identified and addressed when good governance is in place.

7.4.2. Senior Management Responsibility

Directors, executives, and senior managers are ultimately responsible for the success of organizational projects and business strategy.

While responsibility for some aspects of projects may be delegated to others, senior managers remain accountable for effective, efficient, and acceptable use of organizational resources.

Ensuring adequate oversight of significant projects is important for being informed and maintaining accountability.

7.4.3. Sound Investment Decisions

Good project governance, including effective communications and accessible escalation procedures, helps an organization ensure that its investments contribute positively to overall organizational performance through:

- Giving priority to projects that have the greatest value to the organization and align with business objectives.
- Requiring that projects deliver all elements of change necessary to achieve desired outcomes, especially with regard to people, process, structure, and technology.

7.5. The Impact of Poor Governance

According to *A Review of Project Governance Effectiveness in Australia* (Caravel Group, 2013) an average of 48% of projects fail to meet their baseline time, cost, and quality objectives. While the project team is more often than not blamed, it is believed the actual cause of failure comes down to a lack of governance. The following table from Caravel's review illustrates the impact of governance basics on the success of projects.

Success Criteria	Yes	No
Approved governance plans exist	13%	87%
Governance team member position descriptions have project governance KPIs	17%	83%
Governance team member performance is measured	6%	94%
Governance team performance is measured	9%	91%
Project governance skills adequate	20%	80%
Governance team members have no conflicts of interest	30%	70%
Governance team and project team have adequate financial authority	45%	55%
Governance team members exhibit proper corporate behavior	45%	55%
Governance team understand difference between business consultants, solution subject matter experts (SMEs), and project delivery SMEs	30%	70%

Table 7-1: Impact of Governance on Project Success

Other common governance issues are outlined below.

Type of issue	Examples
Sponsor	▪ Tendency to over control, acting as a "super project manager " not a sponsor ▪ Not working at the right proximity — too close or too remote to the team ▪ Failing to attend the kick-off meeting and having no involvement in the project ▪ Lack of time to attend meetings and provide other support ▪ Manipulating and unduly influencing the team in the belief they know the right plan ▪ Not sharing — not believing in the team and failing to share thoughts/ideas ▪ Not properly communicating to the project team changing organizational priorities and objectives ▪ Not properly advocating for the project to the organization and senior management
Project manager	▪ Avoiding the sponsor — due to not understanding the sponsor role, feeling intimidated, or a mismatch or lack of agreement with the sponsor on project objectives ▪ Being caught in the middle — feeling bad because the team are working in one direction, and the sponsor wants the project to take a different direction, or a mismatch or lack of agreement with the sponsor on project objectives ▪ Not working out in the project manager role, perhaps because of inexperience or the wrong skills ▪ Burnout due to workload or lack of support from the sponsor ▪ Lack of business and technical experience in the disciplines of the project
Ambiguity	▪ Lack of role clarity ▪ Poor project chartering ▪ Lack of understanding of specific roles ▪ Business cases not being prepared or approved ▪ Business case being continuously revisited and modified
Portfolio level	▪ Too many projects being run ▪ Insufficient resources to meet current resource demands ▪ Project selection model or process does not take into account current or changing organizational requirements ▪ Insufficient communications and escalation from the project teams to update the portfolio, and insufficient communications from the organization to the project teams

Table 7-2: Common Governance Issues

7.6. Governance of Project Management Roles

The particular roles needed for effective governance will vary depending on your organization and the project. Typical roles are outlined below.

7.6.1. Project Management Offices

Project Management Offices (PMOs) play a key role in the governance of projects. The overall intention of the PMO is to ensure that the right decisions are taken by the right people (or group) based on the right level of supporting information. There should be a single source for any piece of data. While each PMO operates under a unique charter, most PMOs perform roles such as:

- Ensuring outputs meet requirements.
- Helping balance conflicting priorities/resources.
- Guiding the project team.
- Fostering positive communication outside of the committee about the project's progress and outcomes.
- Reviewing project progress.
- Providing appropriate resources and specializations to the project teams.
- Checking adherence of project activities against standards of best-practice making and enforcing decisions.

7.6.2. Project Sponsor

The project or program sponsor plays a critical role in the governance of individual projects and programs. They:

- Own, develop, and maintain the project business case.
- Engage with peers in the organization to manage relationships and politics.
- Serve as a focus point for decisions beyond the project manager's scope of authority.
- Act swiftly and decisively to resolve conflicts.
- Reinforce project management principles and methodology.
- Review the viability of a project against critical success criteria at stage and phase gates.
- Accept project deliverables at handover and project close-out.
- Conduct benefits realization reviews.

The sponsor performs different roles during the project lifecycle, including the roles of:

- Supplier
- Coach and mentor
- Filter
- Business judge
- Motivator
- Negotiator
- Protector
- Link to upper management

There are number of desired behaviors of project sponsors. These are described in the table below.

Category	Desired Behaviors
Relationship and selling	▪ Actively develop and manage relationships with peers in the client and the organization ▪ Proactively manage politics, keeping relationships going through an engagement ▪ Position the organization to have significant long-term business relationships
Leadership	▪ Serve as a focal point for decisions beyond the project manager's scope of authority ▪ Be proactively involved throughout the duration of the project ▪ Lead for results and success by conveying a sense of urgency ▪ Act swiftly and decisively to resolve conflicts
Project Management	▪ Reinforce application of project management principles and the use of PM methodology ▪ Review and monitor project scope and risk ▪ Promote knowledge creation and reuse
Consulting engagement	▪ Understanding the big picture and the effect of the solution on the client ▪ Identify areas of change and resistance in the client organization and alert the project manager
Business management	▪ Understand and plan for risk across the business ▪ Coach others on the management of risk ▪ Understand the implications and cost base for the solution

Table 7-3: Desired Behaviors for Sponsors

7.6.3. *Other Stakeholder Roles*

Other stakeholders also need to be considered when establishing and communicating a governance system. The table below lists some common types of stakeholders and outlines their interests in governance.

Stakeholder Category	Interest
Auditors and regulators	Verifying that an appropriate framework for project governance is provided and implemented
Members of executive boards	Ensuring that the appropriate framework for project governance is created to protect shareholder interests and manage risk
Agents and managers	Assurance that they can implement and work within the identified framework for governance
Senior managers, project sponsors, steering committees, project boards	Having oversight of projects, programs, and portfolios

Stakeholder Category	Interest
Project Management Office staff	Ensuring they can implement the framework for project governance
Project managers	Ensuring they can execute projects within the framework of project governance
Other project stakeholders such as financial investors and special interest groups	Understanding how their interests are being protected
Suppliers	Understanding how their interests are affected

Table 7-4: Stakeholders and their Interests

7.7. Establishing Governance Arrangements

Processes, procedure, people and tools are the ways in which a governance framework is delivered throughout the project lifecycle. Project complexity is a factor in designing appropriate governance, although often cost is a driver too. As explained in earlier modules, one of the challenges as project manager is finding and maintaining the right balance between managing risk and maintaining operational efficiency.

7.7.1. Developing the Governance Plan

Developing, documenting, and communicating a governance plan ensures a shared understanding of the governance standards, roles and responsibilities relevant to the project. Arrangements are sometimes documented within the project plan, or can be the subject of a separate Governance Plan, but should include:

- Clear statements of roles, responsibilities, and performance criteria for the governance of project management, including any delegated authorities for project decisions.
- Authorization points at which the business case is reviewed and approved.
- Specific criteria for reporting project status and for the escalation of risks and issues to the levels required by the organization.
- Who is responsible for deciding when independent scrutiny of projects and project management systems is required, and who implements such scrutiny.
- How project governance integrates with corporate governance.

There may also be requirements for the engagement of project stakeholders to ensure that they are involved at a level that is commensurate with their importance to the organization and in a manner that fosters trust. Governance arrangements also frequently seek to ensure that the organization fosters a culture of improvement, of the ability to escalate when needed, and of frank internal disclosure of project information.

Delegated authorities can be added to role and position descriptions to reinforce accountability and performance expectations.

These sorts of broad overall requirements are key to the successful governance of all projects within the organization, and it is the project manager 's responsibility to ensure that they are familiar with, and comply with, the appropriate project governance requirements.

7.7.2. Project Steering Committee

As an example of typical governance arrangements, a *project steering committee* within an organization might be responsible for:

- Identifying business priorities based on business plans
- Ensuring projects meet identified business strategies
- Ensuring identified business benefits are delivered
- Delegation of agreed funding
- Monitoring key project milestone achievements
- Reviewing risk control and issue control reports
- Assisting with the resolution of project issues.

7.7.3. Governance Policies and Procedures

Projects also need to be undertaken in ways that align with organizational governance requirements. Mature organizations will have defined governance mechanisms that clarify the responsibilities of different individuals and groups for different aspects of the project. Note however, that existing functional authorities in an organization may not align perfectly to the needs of a project.

Existing governance arrangements might include:

- Overall responsibility for project management vested in a Board of Directors for a private sector organization or in a Departmental Secretary for a government agency.
- Establishment of a Project Steering Committee which may have oversight of all projects, a group of projects, or an individual project
- Purchasing or preferred supplier arrangements
- Communications frameworks and authority to speak on behalf of the project
- Financial delegations

Any existing delegated authorization bodies need to have sufficient representation, competence, authority and resources to enable them to make appropriate decisions.

7.8. Summary

Governance is a somewhat abstract concept. However, it is critical to ensure that the right project is delivered in the right way. While the concept was initially focused on the governance of organizations, it has more recently been applied to projects. Governance of project management is critical to sustainable projects as it ensures that project sponsors are making the right decisions in a timely manner.

For a sustainable project manager, working effectively with the project sponsor is a must. However, not all sponsors are experienced in sponsoring projects, so it is critical to manage upwards and where necessary, to put in place appropriate governance arrangements for the project.

8. Benefits Management

The real conflict is not between profit maximization and social responsibility ... but rather between short- and long-term thinking. (Schwab)

In Chapter 2, we defined a *project* as an investment undertaken to obtain a desired outcome. In Chapter 4, we defined *project success* as a combination of project management success and product success. In this chapter, we will tie those two ideas together under the heading of *benefits management*: benefits are both the desired outcome of our definition and the way we measure product success.

To ensure success, sustainable project managers must take a long-term perspective. Although the project team members may not be accountable for benefits realization, they are in the perfect position to improve benefits by reducing operational costs, limiting negative environmental impacts, and improving acceptance and adoption of the project deliverables.

In a study of construction projects done by *ENR* several years ago, over 40% of projects were late and more than 50% were over budget, yet nearly 90% of owners were satisfied with the results because of the benefits obtained.

It's important for the entire project team to remember that benefits are the reason for the project.

8.1. Definitions

The following definitions are used in this chapter:

- **Outputs** — are deliverables developed by a project. A deliverable may be a service (e.g., a departmental reorganization) or a tangible product (e.g., working software).
- **Capabilities** — are what an organization can accomplish. New capabilities typically come from combining existing capabilities with the outputs of one or more projects.
- **Outcomes** — are the results of using capabilities.
- **Benefits and Dis-benefits** — are the measurable changes resulting from the outcomes. Benefits and dis-benefits are expected to contribute towards one or more organizational objectives. Different stakeholders may have different views about whether the changes are benefits or dis-benefits.
- **Organizational Changes** — such as new departments, new reporting structures, and new procedures are often need to support new capabilities. Organizational changes may or may not be included within the scope of the project whose delivered capabilities trigger them. Organizational change management is covered in Chapter 9.
- **Side-effects and Consequences** — are secondary changes that occur as a result of the primary organizational change triggered by new capabilities. For example, new policies and procedures could either reduce or increase employee turnover.

Figure 8-1 below (adapted from Axelos, 2011) illustrates the relationships among these terms.

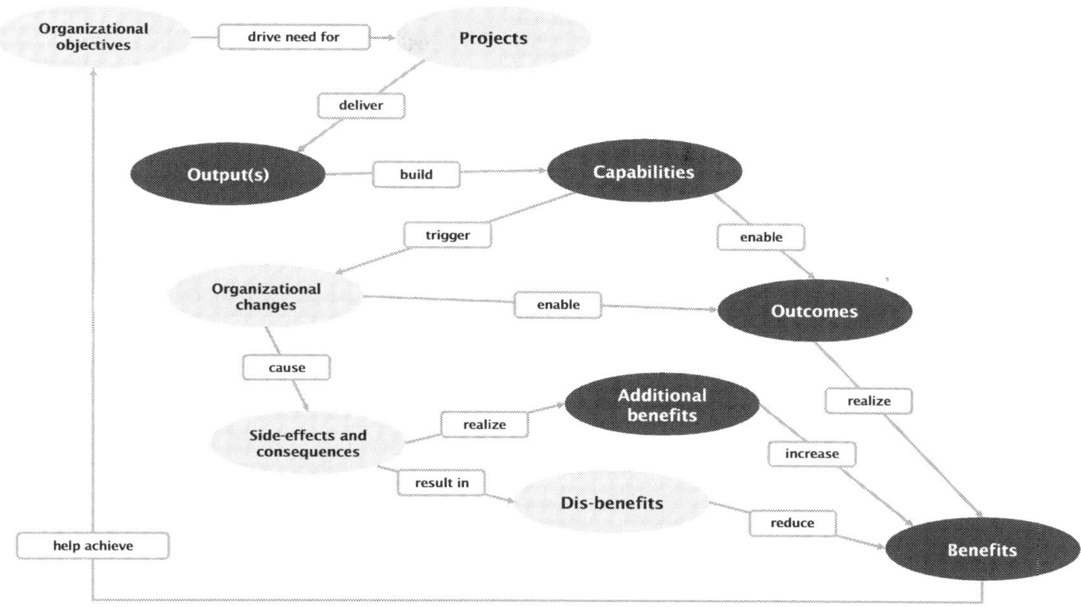

Figure 8-1: Organizational Objectives and Benefits Realization

Notice that the potential for additional benefits and dis-benefits helps to reinforce the importance of regularly updating the business case to help both senior management and the project team make decisions during the project that will maximize benefits.

Table 8-1 below illustrates the major categories of benefits.

Benefit Category	Measures and Indicators
Sustainability	▪ See the P5 ontology in Section 2.3 for a list of areas where a project may generate benefits related to sustainability
Efficiency	▪ Budget reductions ▪ Lower unit cost ▪ Time deployed into other activities ▪ Value of time saved
Cost avoidance	▪ Money recycled to fund the initiative costs ▪ Operating budget reductions ▪ Indicators of what the money saved has been used for
Increased revenue	▪ Sales from new products or services, sales in new markets, higher sales from existing products or services
Revenue retention	▪ Retaining business otherwise lost

Table 8-1: Benefit Categories

8.2. Benefits Management Process

Figure 8-2 below illustrates GPM's recommended process for benefits management.

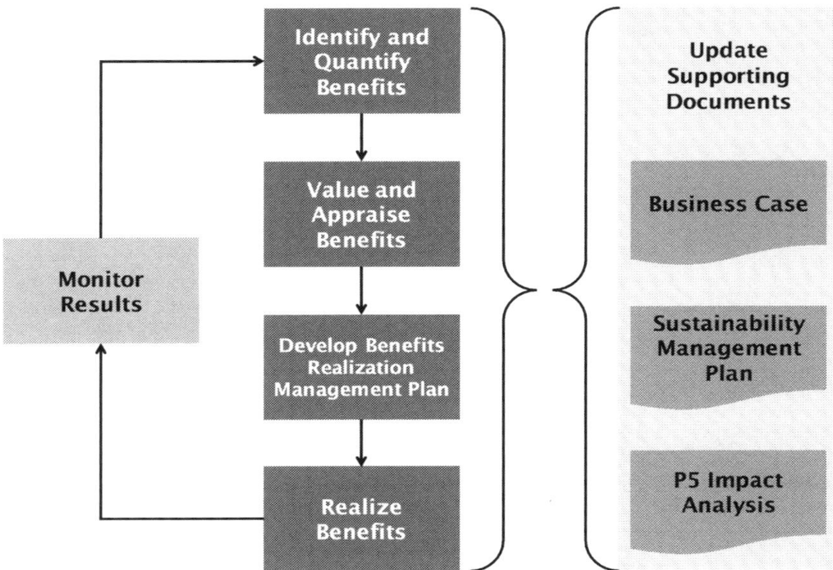

Figure 8-2: Benefits Management Process

The descriptions of the process steps are adapted from Jenner (2014):

Identify and Quantify Benefits. This step would frequently be part of the project activities and might include benefits discovery workshops, benefits mapping, voice-of-the-customer sessions, and forecasts of anticipated improvements.

Value and Appraise Benefits. This step involves estimating the monetary and non-monetary value of expected benefits to support alternatives analysis, investment appraisal, and portfolio prioritization. It may include cost-benefit analysis, real options, or multi-criteria analysis.

Develop Benefits Realization Management Plan. This step encompasses validating and prioritizing benefits, assigning ownership, selecting benefits measures, and planning stakeholder engagement.

Realize Benefits. While most benefits will be realized after the project is complete, some benefits may be realized during the project, especially when there are multiple design-and-delivery phases.

Monitor Results. This step provides the basis for learning and improvement before, during, and after the project. It includes the phase-end reviews called for in the PRiSM project lifecycle (see Chapter 4).

Update Supporting Documents. The results of each of the above steps should be incorporated as needed into the Business Case, the Sustainability Management Plan, and the P5 Impact Analysis. These documents are also described in more detail in Chapter 4.

8.3. Sustainability and Benefits Management

One of the fundamental assumptions of sustainable project management is that a project is part of a product lifecycle that runs cradle-to-cradle. This is shown in Figure 8-3 below. This figure illustrates the importance of benefits management by showing that for most projects, project costs are relatively small in comparison to the benefits expected. The figure also suggests that a sustainable project manager must be aware of the long-term impact of their project decisions.

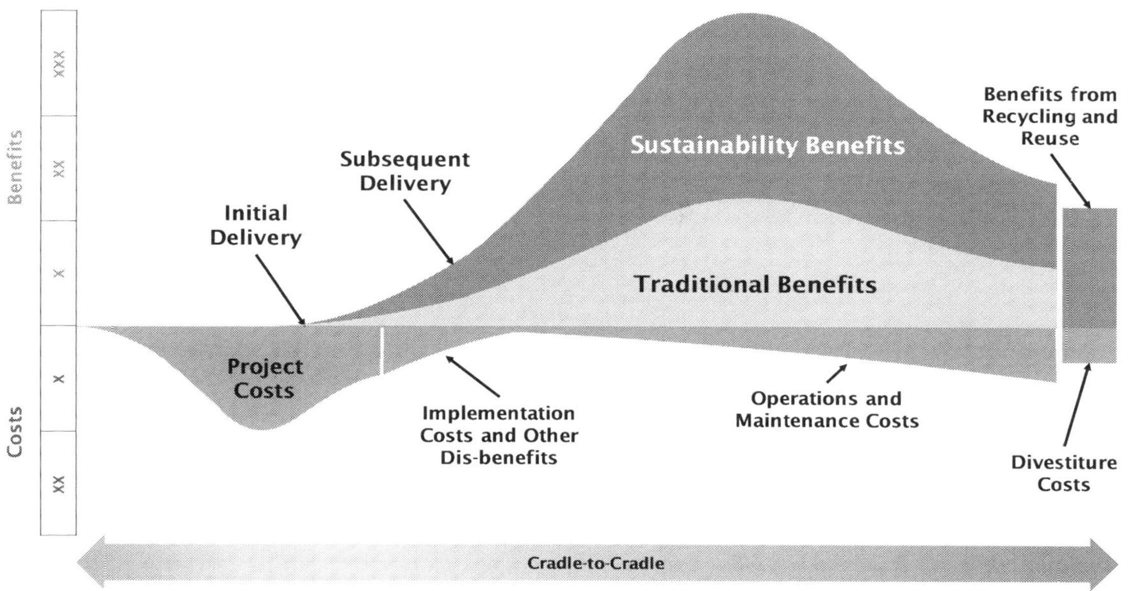

Figure 8-3: Cradle-to-Cradle Lifecycle

One important question related to this topic is the role of the project manager (and the project management team) in benefits realization. Most organizations assign accountability for benefits realization to the sponsor and ask the project manager to focus exclusively on the project's outputs. The rationale for this position is that the project manager is not involved in what happens after project completion.

However, project managers (and the project management team) clearly have the ability to influence benefits realization through their decisions about how to resolve problems, how to respond to risks, and how to develop the project's outputs. For example, cutting corners during the project to save money and meet the budget target could result in a low quality product that fails to deliver the expected revenues.

GPM's position is that the project team must consider the impact of their decisions on the acceptance, adoption, and integration of the project outputs into a new capability to help ensure sustainability and benefits realization.

8.4. Additional Benefits of Benefits Management

Good benefits management helps support a number of different organizational and project areas as shown in Figure 8-4 below. Benefits management can help support and empower other disciplines such as project portfolio management, risk management, project planning, and stakeholder engagement.

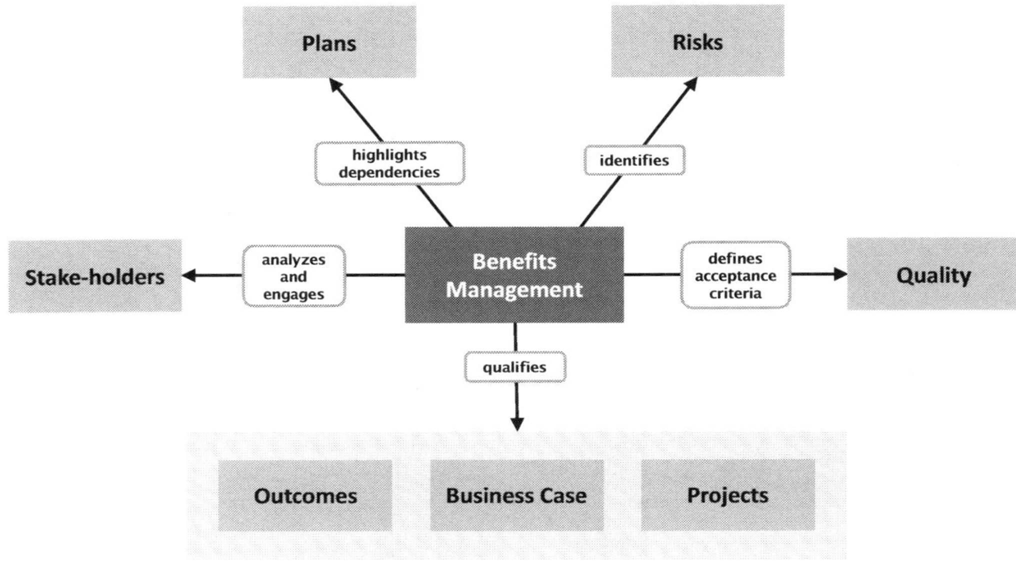

Figure 8-4: Benefits Management Interfaces

In short, benefits management isn't simply a nice-to-have component of project management. Benefits management is the primary purpose for the investment in the project and a key supporting discipline for all other project disciplines.

8.5. Summary

This chapter focused on project benefits and ensuring that the realization of benefits is planned and managed throughout the project. Benefits may be as simple as avoiding costs or as complex as becoming more efficient through implementation of an enterprise resource planning system.

Achieving sustainable outcomes is the ultimate benefit from a sustainable project. To be truly sustainable, benefits must accrue to groups outside the organization such as a specific ecosystem or subset of the economy.

The challenge for sustainable project managers is that the intended benefits may not be realizable for months or even years after the project is finished. This can make it difficult for the sustainable project manager to make good decisions about those expected benefits.

Notes

9. Organizational Change Management

Organizational change management (OCM) is the practice of applying a structured approach to transition an organization from its current state to a desired future state to achieve expected benefits (ACMP, 2014). It includes supporting both the organization itself and the individuals who comprise the organization. OCM is both a repeatable process used to drive a successful change process, and a set of skills for leaders that creates a capacity for increasing organizational effectiveness.

Organizational changes can affect the entire organization or a subset such as a business unit, a department, or a location. Extreme changes are often called *transformations*. The concepts in this chapter apply to all types of organizational change.

OCM can be delivered as part of the scope of a project, as the entire scope of a project, or as part of ongoing operations. In this chapter, we are mostly concerned with OCM when it is part of a project.

OCM is sometimes called *change management*. However, in the project context, change management also refers to managing changes to requirements, specifications, plans, and other aspects of the project. To ensure clarity, we will consistently refer to OCM when discussing changes in the organization or its employees.

9.1. The Organizational Change Management Process

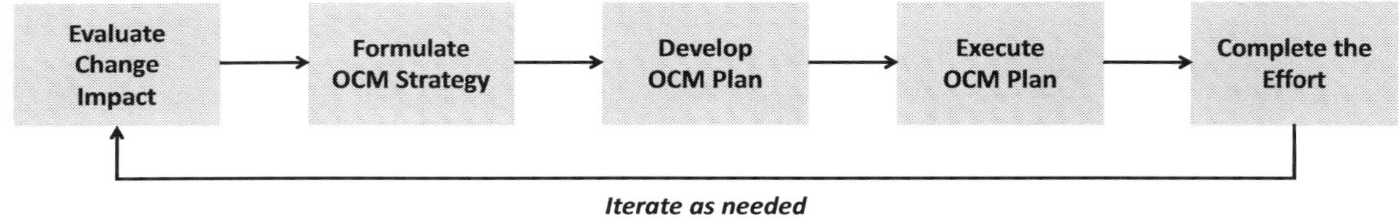

Figure 9-1: The Organizational Change Management Process

The organizational change management process is illustrated in Figure 9-1 above and briefly described in the paragraphs below:

- **Evaluate Change Impact.** This step involves evaluating the organization's readiness and capacity to undergo a transition from the current state to its desired future state. The evaluation results provide change practitioners with information to calibrate leader expectations and to scale and customize change management plans and activities.
- **Formulate OCM Strategy.** This step involves determining how to incorporate, integrate, and align change management plans, activities, and milestones into the existing operations of an organization. Of particular concern when developing an OCM strategy is the timing and sequence of the changes.
- **Develop OCM Plan.** The OCM plan should include communications, sponsorship, stakeholder engagement, learning and development, risk management, and measurement and benefits realization.

- **Execute OCM Plan.** This is when the expected benefits of the change are realized. Both strategy and plans may be modified based on interim results.
- **Complete the Effort.** This step is similar to PRiSM's closure phase. It includes measuring results and comparing them to the expected benefits.

9.1.1. Principles of Leading OCM

The following list of ten guiding principles for change can help executives who are committed to effecting organizational change (Strategy, 2014).

Principle 1: Lead with the culture. Human beings with strong emotional connections to the culture will be enacting these changes. To use this emotional energy, leaders must look for the elements of the culture that are aligned to the change, bring them to the foreground, and attract the attention of the people who will be affected by the change.

Principle 2: Start at the top. All successful organizational change management initiatives start at the top, with a committed and well-aligned group of executives strongly supported by the CEO. Work must be done in advance to ensure that everyone agrees about the case for the change and the particulars for implementing it.

Principle 3: Involve every layer. Frontline people tend to be rich repositories of knowledge about where potential glitches may occur, what technical and logistical issues need to be addressed, and how customers may react to changes. In addition, their full-hearted engagement can smooth the way for complex change initiatives, whereas their resistance will make implementation an ongoing challenge.

Principle 4: Make the rational and emotional case together. Leaders will often make the case for major change on the sole basis of strategic business objectives such as "we will enter new markets." Such objectives rarely reach people emotionally in a way that ensures genuine commitment to the cause. Human beings respond to calls to action that engage their hearts as well as their minds, making them feel as if they're part of something consequential.

Principle 5: Act your way into new thinking. Many organizational change initiatives seem to assume that people will begin to shift their behaviors once formal elements like directives and incentives have been put in place, and that managers will become clear communicators because they have a mandate to deliver a message about the change. More critical to the success of any organizational change initiative is ensuring that people's daily behaviors reflect the imperative of change. Start by defining a critical few behaviors that will be essential to the success of the initiative. Senior leaders must visibly model these new behaviors themselves, right from the start, because employees will only believe real change is occurring when they see it happening at the top of the organization.

Principle 6: Engage, engage, engage. Powerful and sustained change requires constant communication, not only throughout the rollout but after the major elements of the plan are in place. The more kinds of communication employed, the more effective they are.

Principle 7: Lead outside the lines. Change has the best chance of cascading through an organization when everyone with authority and influence is involved. This group includes people whose power is more informal and is related to their expertise, to the breadth of their network, or to personal qualities that engender trust. They are sometimes called *special forces* or *thought leaders*. They can be found throughout any organization. They might include a well-respected field supervisor, an innovative project manager, or a receptionist who's been at their post for 25 years. There are three distinct kinds of such informal leaders:

- *Pride builders* are great at motivating others and inspiring them to take pride in their work.
- *Trusted nodes* are go-to people. They are repositories of the organization's culture. They are the ones approached by people who want to know what's really happening in the organization.
- *Change* or *culture ambassadors* know, as if by instinct, how to live the change the organization is making. They serve as both exemplars and communicators, spreading the word about why change is important.

Principle 8: Leverage formal solutions. Persuading people to change their behavior won't suffice unless formal elements such as structure, reward systems, ways of operating, training, and development are redesigned to support them.

Principle 9: Leverage informal solutions. Even when the formal elements needed for organizational change are present, the established culture can undermine them if people revert to long-held but unconscious ways of behaving. This is why formal and informal solutions must work together. A top-tier technology company was trying to inculcate a more customer-centric mind-set after a decade focused on relentlessly cutting costs. The slogan of the cost-cutting era, "Ship by any means," was replaced by a new one: "If it's not right, don't ship it." By asking people at every level to be responsible for quality — and by celebrating and rewarding improvements — change leaders were able to create an ethic of ownership in the product.

Principle 10: Assess and adapt. Leaders are often so eager to claim victory that they don't take the time to find out what's working and what's not, and to adjust their next steps accordingly. This failure results in inconsistency and deprives the organization of needed information about how to support the process of change.

9.1.2. The Importance of Culture

In 2013, The Katzenbach Center undertook a study to identify the main barriers to successful organizational change. They surveyed 2,200 global senior executives and found a strong correlation between the success of organizational change programs and whether culture was leveraged in the change process:

- When change initiatives succeeded, 56% said their organizations used the existing culture as a source of energy and influence, and 70% said their organizations tried to leverage their employees' pride in, and emotional commitment to, their organizations.
- When change initiatives fell short, 24% said their organizations had used the existing culture as a source of energy and influence, and 35% said their organizations tried to leverage their employees' pride in, and emotional commitment to, their organizations.

The survey also showed that:

- Only 54% of major organizational change initiatives succeeded.
- 86% of C-suite executives and 84% of managers and employees said culture was critical to their organization's success.
- 65% said they had experienced some form of *change fatigue* (a dynamic that comes into play when employees feel they are being asked to make too many changes at once).
- 48% said their companies didn't have the necessary capabilities to ensure that change is sustained.
- 44% of employees said they didn't understand the change they were being asked to make, and 38% said they didn't agree with it.

9.2. Sustainability and OCM

Becoming sustainable is one example of organizational change, and as such, it requires organizational change management. Becoming sustainable requires leaders to articulate a consistent, achievable, inspiring, and easily understood *vision* that guides the organization to measurable achievement of expected benefits.

A vision is an aspirational and future-focused statement. A vision statement creates the link between strategic planning and organizational change management by:

- Providing clarity of direction and focus for the organization and stakeholders.
- Identifying high-level results and expected benefits to be achieved.
- Setting the stage for leaders to align stakeholders to a common plan.
- Being a guide for decision making, communications, and engagement.

For sustainability to be fully embedded in core business practices means aligning the corporate vision and strategy with sustainability objectives and setting business targets that drive these broader values. Leading companies treat sustainability both as a shared responsibility and as an opportunity, accompanied by proactive strategies that drive change through market-changing ideas and products and by investing in technological innovation and new business models.

9.3. Change Models

Change models address both organizational change and individual change. Sustainable project managers are likely to need to deal with both. Table 9-1 provides an overview of several of the better-known change models.

Model Name	Major Components	When to Use
Lewin's Model	▪ Unfreeze ▪ Change ▪ Refreeze	When massive changes to processes and practice are needed throughout the organization.
McKinsey 7-S model	▪ Strategy ▪ Structure ▪ Systems ▪ Shared values ▪ Style ▪ Staff ▪ Skills	To determine what changes are needed by analyzing where the seven items fail to support each other.
Kotter	▪ Create a sense of urgency ▪ Build a core coalition ▪ Form a strategic vision ▪ Get everyone on board ▪ Remove barriers and reduce friction ▪ Generate short-term wins ▪ Sustain acceleration ▪ Set the changes in stone	When you need a checklist about what has to be done and in what order.

Model Name	Major Components	When to Use
Nudge Theory	▪ Clearly define your changes ▪ Consider changes from your employees' point of view ▪ Use evidence to show the best option ▪ Present the change as a choice ▪ Listen to feedback ▪ Limit obstacles ▪ Keep momentum up with short-term wins	When employee buy-in is particularly important. Basic concept relies on convincing individuals to make the choice to change rather than imposing it from above.
Bridges' Transition Model	▪ Ending, losing, and letting go ▪ The neutral zone ▪ The new beginning	When changes will be accomplished slowly.
Kübler-Ross Change Curve	▪ Denial ▪ Anger ▪ Bargaining ▪ Depression ▪ Acceptance	When dealing with emotions is very important to accomplishing change.
ADKAR	▪ Awareness (of the need to change) ▪ Desire (to participate and support the change) ▪ Knowledge (on how to change) ▪ Ability (to implement required skills and behaviors) ▪ Reinforcement (to sustain the change)	When a bottom-up approach focused on the employees is needed.

Table 9-1: Overview of OCM Models

Of the above models, the Prosci change management model ADKAR is probably the best known within the project management community. It is a goal-oriented model that can be used to guide both individual and organizational change. ADKAR is an acronym that represents the five outcomes an individual or organization must achieve for change to be successful: awareness, desire, knowledge, ability, and reinforcement as illustrated in Figure 9-2 below:

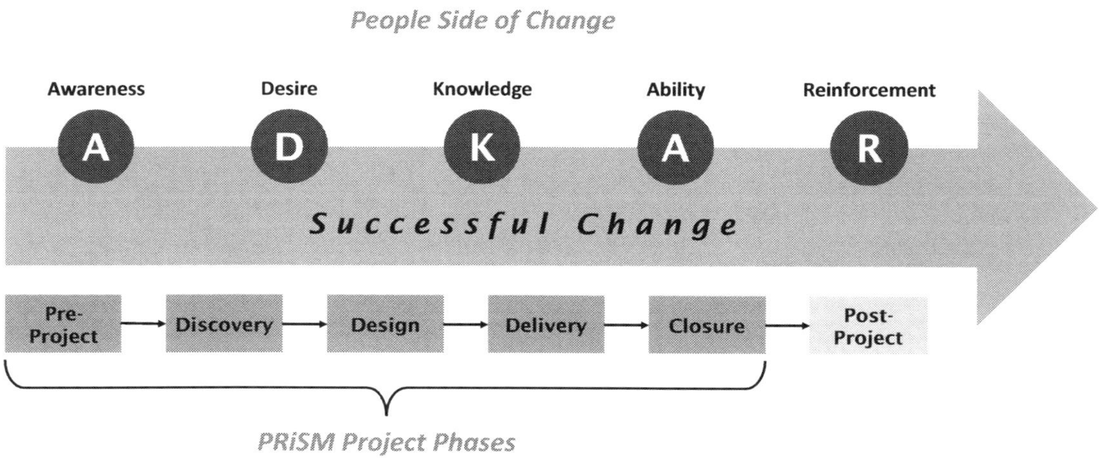

Figure 9-2: ADKAR Model

Awareness of the business reasons for change. Why is it necessary to change? Awareness is the goal/ outcome of early communications related to an organizational change. As potential resistance factors might include: comfort with the status quo, denial that the reasons for change are real, credibility of the source or sender of the message, rumors, or misinformation.

Desire to engage and participate in the change. Desire is the goal/ outcome of sponsorship and resistance management. Potential resisting factors might include comfort or security with how things are now, change not aligned with a person's self-interest or values, or an individual's personal situation — financial, career, family, health.

Knowledge about how to change. Actually, there are two distinct types of knowledge. The first is knowledge on how to change (what to do during the transition), and the second is knowledge on how to perform effectively in the future state (knowledge on the ultimate skills and behaviors needed to support the change). Knowledge is the goal/outcome of training and coaching. As potential resisting factors might include: gap between current and desired knowledge levels, knowledge levels, inadequate resources available for training, lack of access to the necessary information, insufficient time, capacity to learn.

Ability to realize or implement the change at the required performance level. Ability is the goal/outcome of additional coaching, practice and time. As potential resisting factors might include: lack of support, inadequate time available to develop skills, psychological blocks, limitations in physical abilities, existing habits contrary to the desired behavior

Reinforcement to ensure change sticks. The focus on reinforcement needs to remain strong so that changes are sustained and deliver the expected results over time. Reinforcement is the goal/outcome of adoption measurement, corrective action and recognition of successful change. As potential resisting factors might include: rewards not meaningful or not associated with achievement, negative consequences including peer pressure for desired behavior.

9.4. OCM and Project Management

Project management and change management are complementary and interdependent disciplines that may overlap when delivering value to the organization, the society, and the environment.

Effective integration of project management and change management is required to ensure that organizational objectives are achieved. Integration can occur across various dimensions:

Area	Project Management of OCM Initiatives	Organizational Change Management
Focus	Application of skills, tools, and techniques to activities required to deliver support for the change (such as new systems, new processes, new resources).	Application of skills, tools, and techniques required to implement and sustain the desired change (such as influencing individual behavior and organizational culture, facilitating new ways of working, and tracking and enabling benefits realization).

Area	Project Management of OCM Initiatives	Organizational Change Management
Approaches	Organization and management of resources and activities required to deliver support for the change.	Activities required to prepare the organization for the change, facilitate the transition from the old way of working to the desired future state, and embed the change as the new norm.
Risk Focus	Threats to schedule, scope, and budget.	Threats to adoption of the change, realization of the expected benefits, and institutionalizing the change.
Objectives and Outcomes	Add value to the organization, to the environment, and to society.	

Table 9-2: Project Management and OCM

9.5. Summary

Organizational change management is the discipline of managing the change in behaviors of people and their working practices. This chapter explores organizational change management and describes key principles that underpin effective OCM. It also provides some details about the Prosci ADKAR model. Ultimately, organizational change involves changing people and their habits and routines. While a sustainable project manager can adopt best-practice models, it may still be a challenging to overcome resistance or an individual's reluctance to do something different.

Notes

10. Value Management

There is nothing so useless as doing efficiently that which should not be done at all.
(Peter F. Drucker)

Value management, also called *value engineering* or *value analysis*, supports sustainable project management because it helps the project team design and develop outputs that deliver the desired outcomes while minimizing negative environmental, economic, and social impacts and creating positive ones. When done well, it also helps to obtain consensus and buy-in.

The foundational concepts of value management were initially developed at General Electric after World War II in response to material shortages. Instead of asking "how can we find alternative sources of materials," GE's engineers asked, "what function does this component perform and how else can we perform that function?" Basically, value management promotes the substitution of materials and methods with more sustainable alternatives, without sacrificing functionality.

Value management helps to ensure that the project's outputs will be suited to their intended purpose. With value management, the focus is on what things *do* rather than on what things *are:* on the *outcomes* or *functions* rather than the *outputs*. As illustrated in Figure 10-1, a house is an output with an outcome of safety and protection.

Figure 10-1: Value Management Focuses on Functionality

10.1. Definitions

The following definitions are adapted from *Management of Value* (Axelos, 2010):

- **Value** — the benefits delivered in proportion to the resources put into acquiring them. Note that this is the inverse of the traditional cost-benefit ratio.
- **Value Management** — a systematic method to maximize value from a project.

- **Function** — a description of what something does, expressed as an active verb and a measurable noun (e.g., bears weight). Functions may be organized into a hierarchy. Functions that relate directly to the expected project outcomes are called primary functions.
- **Value Driver** — a primary function. Value drivers, in aggregate, are sufficient to achieve the project outcomes in full.

10.2. The Benefits of Value Management

Value management provides benefits in two major areas:

- It can have a major impact on the economic, social, and environmental whole-life costs of the outputs of the project.
- Applying it early in the project can help to avoid the high cost of later changes.

The cost of constructing and occupying a building includes building construction costs, building operating costs, and business operating costs. Of these three, the building construction costs (project costs) are the lowest by far (Fuller, 2016) as illustrated in Figure 10-2. By using value management to make design choices that support more efficient and effective business operations, the impact of the project on the environmental, economic, and social factors identified in P5 may be greatly reduced.

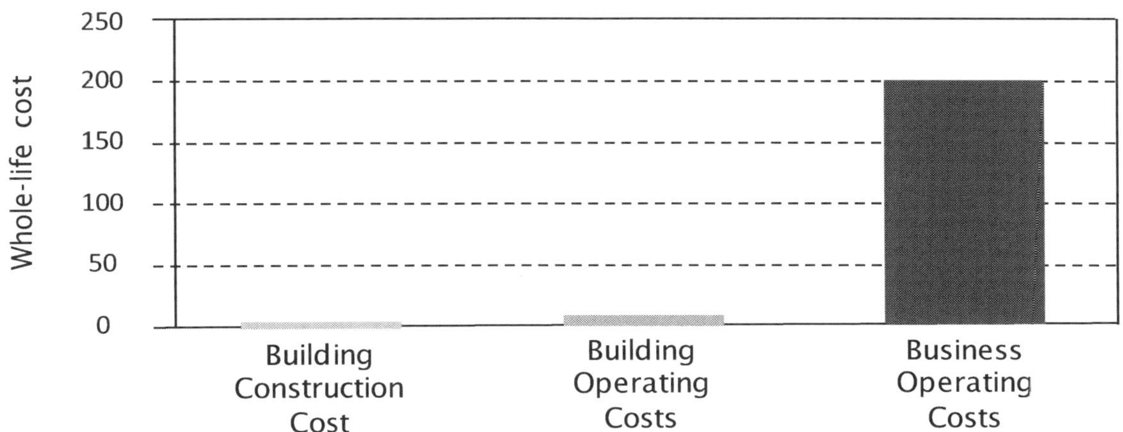

Figure 10-2: Whole-life Cost of a Building

Employing value management early on can help mitigate the cost of late changes. As illustrated below in Figure 10-3, changes that are made later in the project lifecycle invariably cost more to implement. For example, changing the door design for a new airplane after tooling has begun would cost much more than the same change made during the design phase.

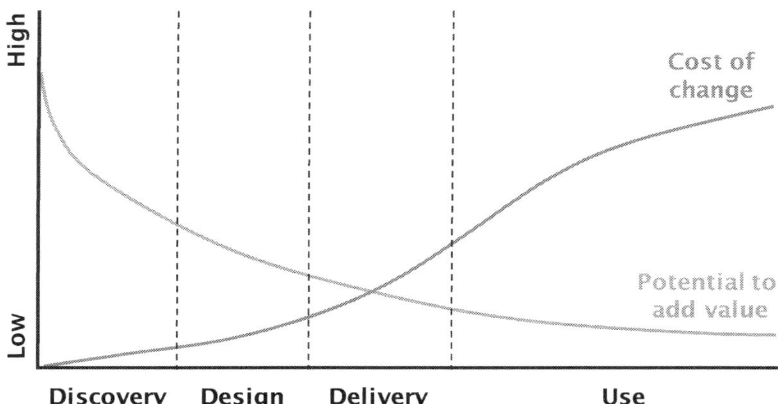

Figure 10-3: Timing and Cost of Change

10.3. Value Management Requires Trade-offs

As illustrated in Figure 10-4, there are three areas where it is necessary to strike a balance by making trade-offs:

- Balancing benefits and expenditures
- Balancing stakeholder needs
- Balancing the use of resources

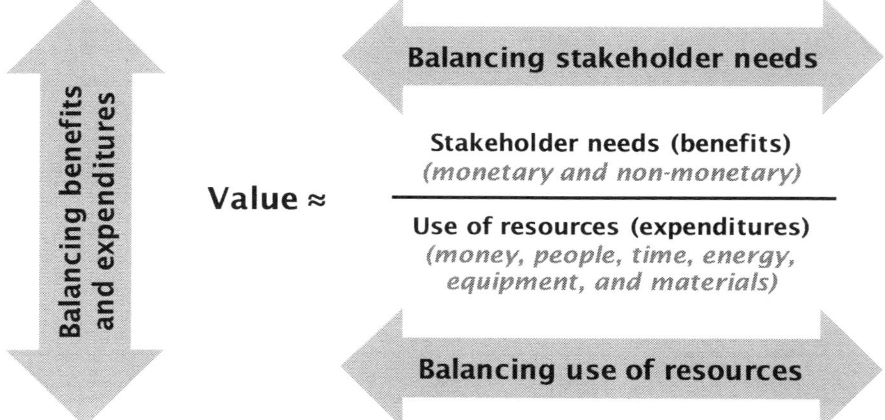

Figure 10-4: Balancing the Variables to Maximize Value

As an example, consider the case of a proposed new park. Local residents were polled about their desires and priorities while the municipality developed estimates of construction cost and annual operating cost. This information is shown in Table 10-1 below.

Function	Main Beneficiaries	Priority	Construction Cost	Operating Cost
Wood play structure	Young children and their parents	1	60,000	10,000
Athletic field	Teens, adults	2	22,000	15,000
Protective Fence	All users, maintenance department	3	20,000	2,000
Wash rooms	Young children and their parents	4	15,000	20,000
Water for drinking	All residents	5	8,000	2,000
Internet access	All residents	6	10,000	3,000
		Totals	**135,000**	**52,000**

Table 10-1: Proposed Park Features and Costs

The municipality had 120,000 budgeted for construction and 30,000 for annual maintenance. Based on those constraints, the initial proposal was to omit the wash rooms and to cut back on maintenance of the athletic field.

Through value management, the municipality identified the following options:

- Ask the users of the athletic fields to do some of the maintenance: delivering the same functionality for less cost by using a different mix of resources.
- Build a larger play structure suitable for older children by using PVC pipe: delivering more functionality for the same cost.
- Using PVC pipe would also involve balancing the needs of the different stakeholders: some parents would be happier and others would be less happy.

10.4. Value Management Process

Since value management is mostly about making design choices, the Pre-Project, Discovery, and Design Phases of the PRiSM project lifecycle would be the ones most affected as shown in Figure 10-5:

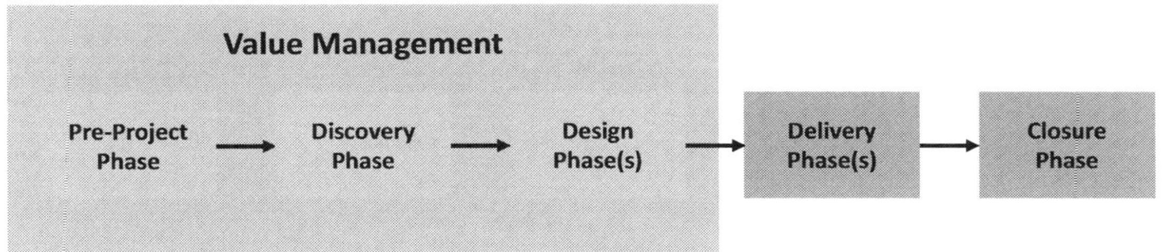

Figure 10-5: Value Management in the PRiSM Project Lifecycle

Within each phase, the business case, sustainability management plan, and P5 impact analysis would be updated as needed based on the results of any value analysis. The steps shown in Figure 10-6 are described below.

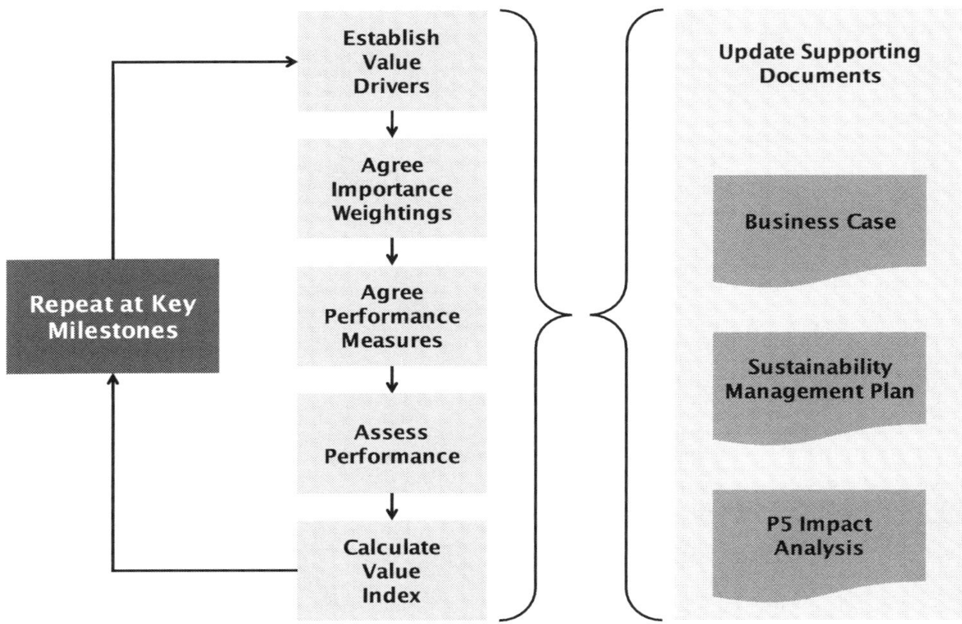

Figure 10-6: Value Measurement Process (VAMP)

Establish Value Drivers. This step involves documenting the features and characteristics (functions) of the expected project outputs so that they can used to perform value analysis. GPM suggests using the Function Analysis System Technique (FAST) which is described below.

Agree Importance Weightings. This step involves determining how important each function is to the stakeholders. GPM recommends getting the key stakeholders involved through a fair process as described below.

Agree Performance Measures. This step involves deciding what metrics to use to determine if the function is being provided effectively and efficiently.

Assess Performance. This step involves using the performance measures to rate each of the functions.

Calculate Value Index. The value index is the weight times the rating divided by the cost. High values indicate good value for the money.

Repeat at Key Milestones. Typically, this would be done at the end of each project lifecycle phase.

10.5. Stakeholder Involvement

Since value management is intended to increase stakeholder satisfaction with the project results, it makes sense to get the stakeholders involved in the process. One proven approach is *fair process.*

Research on stakeholder involvement (Kim & Mauborgne, 2003) has shown that:

- People care about the decisions that affect them, but they care even more about the process used to make those decisions.
- Most people will accept decisions not wholly in their favor if they believe the process for arriving at those decisions was fair.
- People may actually dislike a positive decision if they do not trust the process used to make that decision.

The steps in the fair process approach are as follows:

- **Engagement** — involving individuals in decisions by inviting their input and encouraging them to challenge one another's ideas. Engagement communicates respect for individuals and their ideas and builds collective wisdom. It generates better decisions and greater commitment from those involved in executing those decisions.
- **Explanation** — clarifying the thinking behind a final decision. Explanations reassure people that their opinions have been considered. With a clear explanation, individuals are more likely to trust the decision-maker's intentions even if their own ideas were rejected.
- **Expectation clarity — clearly** stating the implications of the decisions and choices made. In particular, stakeholders need to be made aware of the impact on them.

Fair process does not require unanimity. Fair process does not set out to achieve harmony or to win people's support through compromises that accommodate every individual's opinions, needs, or interests. While fair process gives every idea a chance, the merit of the ideas — and not the level of agreement — is what drives the decision making.

Nor is fair process the same as democracy in the workplace. Using fair process does not mean that managers forfeit their prerogative to make decisions. Fair process pursues the best ideas whether they are put forth by one or many, or by someone in or out of power.

10.6. Establishing Value Drivers

One approach to *establishing value drivers* is the Function Analysis Systems Technique (FAST). FAST provides a graphical representation of functions and their hierarchy while focusing on customer requirements, interest, expectations, and needs. Figure 10-7 illustrates a FAST hierarchy arranged left-to-right rather than top-to-bottom.

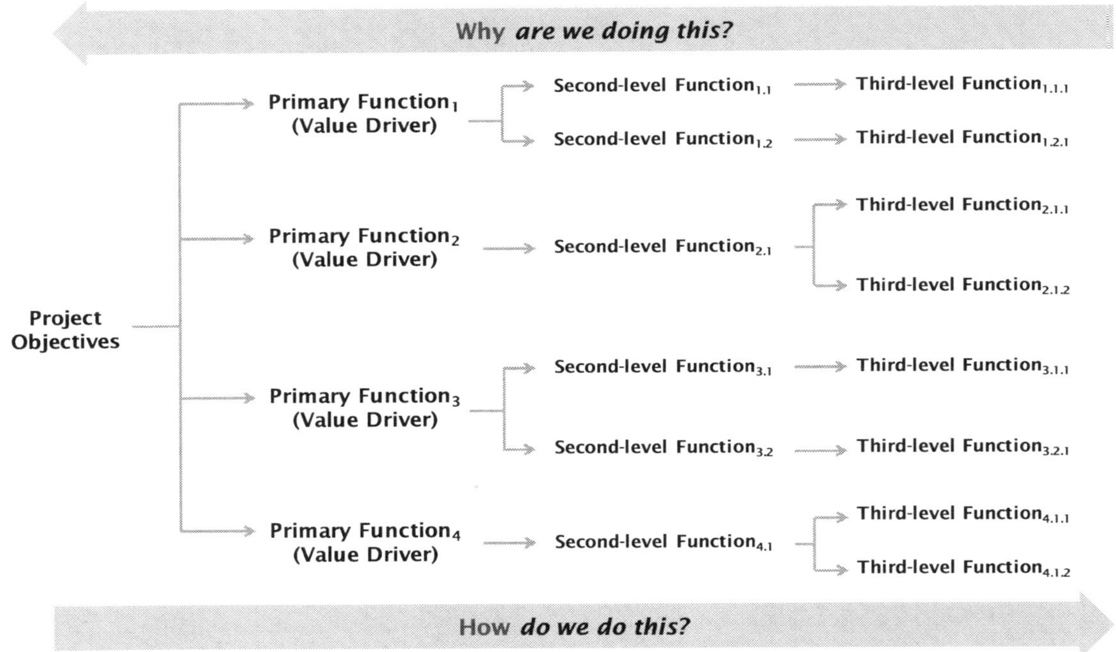

Figure 10-7: Function Analysis System Technique Diagram

A FAST diagram for a primary function of *eliminating mice* might look something like this:

Primary Function (Value Driver)	Second-Level Functions	Third-Level Functions	Fourth-Level Functions	Fifth-Level Functions
Eliminate mice	Kill mouse	Trigger striker	Attract mouse	Bait trap
	Buy cat	n/a	n/a	n/a

Table 10-2: FAST Diagram for Eliminating Mice

FAST looks at what functions are need to satisfy stakeholder requirements. It does not address the details of how to implement those functions.

10.7. Value Profile

The major uses of the value profile are as follows (OGC, 2010):

- Providing consistency in comparing the relative value of different projects.
- Making decisions based on maximizing value.
- Redistributing resources to where they add the greatest value.

In order to prepare a value profile, the team will need estimates of the cost of each of the value drivers identified in the FAST diagram. If the project team has extensive experience with similar projects, it may be possible to go straight from functions to solutions. If not, an intermediate step of documenting design considerations as illustrated below should be useful.

Why are we doing this

	Project Objective = 200 bed district hospital		
Primary Function (Value Driver)	Limit energy use	Treat in-patients	Facilitate patient access
Secondary Function	Limit heat loss	Treat acute-care patients	Provide access to main entrance
Design Considerations	▪ Control systems ▪ Window size and location ▪ Heat retention	▪ # of beds ▪ Expected # of patients ▪ Equipment installed in room	▪ Location of parking ▪ Size of drop-off area
Design Solutions	▪ Central timers ▪ Energy efficient windows ▪ Thermal curtains ▪ Heat pumps ▪ Underground heat sink	▪ ICU next to ER ▪ 8 bed ICU ▪ Crash cart by each ICU bed	▪ Underground parking garage ▪ Shuttles from remote lot ▪ 5 car drop-off zone

How do we do this?

Figure 10-8: Partial Example of Value Analysis

The team will also need to work with the stakeholders (using fair process or a similar approach) to:

- Establish the relative importance of each function by assigning weights. To allow comparisons of different projects, and to maintain consistency within a single project across multiple iterations, the weights must add up to the same number, usually 100.
- Determine how well the current design satisfies the stakeholders' expectations. This can be done using the rating scale in Table 10-3: Performance Rating Scale or a similar approach.

Score	Description
9–10	***Superior*** — significantly exceeds requirements
7–8	***Good*** — exceeds minimum requirements
4–6	***Average*** — meets minimum requirements
2–3	***Poor*** — barely meets requirements
1	***Unacceptable***

Table 10-3: Performance Rating Scale

The completed value profile shows where to concentrate effort to improve value. In the example below (Table 10-4), the functions in red have the lowest value ratios and are thus prime candidates for trying to reduce the estimated costs. The functions in blue have the highest value ratios so it might be appropriate to consider obtaining additional benefits by spending more to enhance those functions.

Value Driver	Weight	Metric	Rating	Value Score	Cost (millions)	Value Ratio
Limit water and energy use	20	Projected consumption	8	160	18	8.9
Treat in-patients	30	Beds	8	240	120	2.0
Treat out-patients	10	# of physician offices	6	60	60	1.0
Treat emergencies	10	ER size	6	60	25	2.4
Ensure positive patient experience	5	% rooms with outside view	8	40	8	5.0
Support variable patient loads	5	% standard-sized rooms	8	40	6	6.7
Facilitate access to facilities	10	Average distance from parking to main entrance	4	40	12	3.3
Facilitate access between units	10	Average distance between units	7	70	5	14.0
Totals	**100**			**710**	**254**	

Table 10-4: Value Profile for Sample Hospital

10.8. Summary

This chapter explores the concepts of value and value management. It presents an approach to improving the value from a project by focusing on functions (what things do) rather than outputs (what things are). It also emphasizes the importance of getting stakeholders involved in the decision-making process to ensure that they will accept the results.

Notes

11. Systems Thinking

Systems thinking, also called system dynamics, is a discipline for understanding the structures and relationships that underlie how our actions and decisions interact. With roots in disciplines as varied as biology, cybernetics, and ecology, systems thinking provides a useful way of looking at how a sustainable world works. Systems thinking is fundamentally a problem-solving approach that involves identifying variables and their relationships to better understand problems and how to solve them.

11.1. Core Concepts

Systems thinking is built around two *core concepts*: a broad view of what a system is and the importance of feedback loops and time delays in problem solving.

11.1.1. Systems

A *system* is a set of interdependent components working together to achieve a specific objective. A project is a system. A supply chain is a system. A biome is a system. Many project results such as buildings, highways, new consumer products, and software applications are systems.

Systems have several defining characteristics:

- **Purpose.** The purpose describes the expected function of the overall system. The purpose of a project is to deliver the expected result. The purpose of a sustainable project is to do so while enhancing the organization's Triple Bottom Line.
- **Interaction.** A system's components are arranged in a particular way. If they are arranged in a different way, the system will perform either differently or sub-optimally.
- **Interdependence.** If one or more components are missing, the system will either not perform the expected function, or it will perform it sub-optimally.
- **Stability.** A system at or near its normal state is relatively stable and predictable. Conversely, a system that is far from its ideal state can be chaotic and unpredictable.

11.1.2. Feedback Loops and Time Delays

Systems thinking acknowledges the importance of the traditional problem-solving approach of cause-and-effect, but then expands it to include *feedback loops* and *time delays.*

Feedback loops occur when an effect has an impact on the original cause. Feedback loops can be reinforcing (both the cause and the effect are affected in the same way) or balancing (the cause and the effect are affected in opposite ways) as illustrated in Figure 11-1 below.

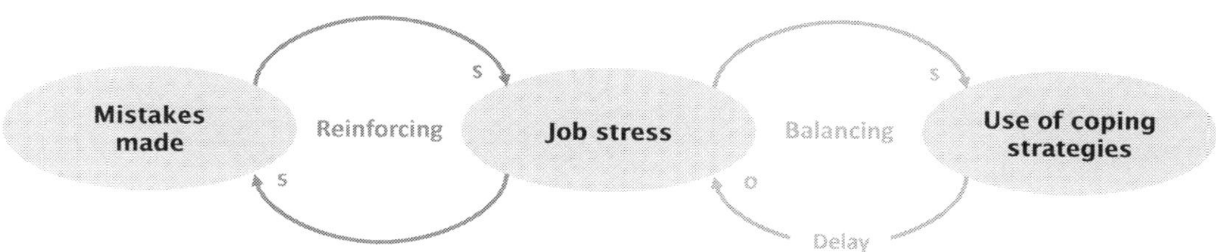

Figure 11-1: Sample Causal Loop Diagram

When the variables change in the *same* direction, we mark the causation arrow with an "s": an increase in job stress causes an increase in mistakes made while a decrease in job stress causes a decrease in mistakes made. At the same time, and increase in mistakes made is likely to increase job stress. This is called a *reinforcing loop* as shown by the loop on the left.

An "o" indicates that the variables change in the *opposite* direction: use of coping strategies causes a reduction in job stress. With one "s" and one "o," the loop is called a *balancing loop* as shown on the right.

The balancing loop in this figure also includes a *delay* to indicate that increased use of coping strategies will not reduce job stress immediately but only after a period of time. The presence of a delay can lead us to believe (erroneously) that the coping strategies are not working.

11.2. Becoming a Systems Thinker

At GPM, we view society, the environment, and the economy as interconnected systems that can be better understood from a systems thinking perspective. As a project manager begins to think about how to accomplish the objectives of the project, these systems need to be considered and addressed, and systems thinking is often the best way to do so.

Senge (1990) suggests that the discipline of systems thinking requires several shifts in how we process information:

- **From parts to the whole.** With any system, the whole is different from the sum of the individual parts. By shifting focus from the parts to the whole, we can better grasp the connections between the different elements.
- **From objects to relationships.** In systems, the relationships between individual parts may be more important than the parts. An ecosystem is not just a collection of species. It also includes living things interacting with each other and their non-living environment.
- **From quantitative to qualitative.** Science has often focused on things that can be measured and quantified. Some aspects of systems, however, like the relationships in a food web, cannot be measured. Rather, they must be mapped.
- **From structure to process.** Living systems develop and evolve. Understanding these systems requires a shift in focus from structures to processes such as evolution, renewal, and change. This may mean that the ways in which decisions are made are as important as the decisions themselves.
- **From contents to patterns.** Within systems, certain configurations of relationships appear again and again in patterns such as cycles and feedback loops. Understanding how a pattern works in one natural or social system helps us to understand other systems that manifest the same pattern.

To be successful in making these shifts, the Waters Foundation (2014) says that systems thinkers:

- Seek to understand the big picture
- Identify the circular nature of complex cause and effect relationships
- Surface and test assumptions
- Consider how mental models affect both the current reality and the future
- Pay attention to accumulations and their rates of change
- Observe how elements within systems change over time, generating patterns and trends
- Make meaningful connections within and between systems
- Use their understanding of system structure to identify possible leverage actions
- Recognize the impact of time delays when exploring cause-and-effect relationships
- Recognize that a system's structure generates its behavior
- Change their perspective to increase understanding
- Consider an issue fully and resist the urge to come to a quick conclusion
- Consider short-term, long-term, and unintended consequences of actions
- Check results and change actions if needed in a process of successive approximation

11.3. Application of Systems Thinking

Systems thinking can help us understand our projects, our society, our environment, and our economy better. This section includes some illustrative examples.

11.3.1. Systems Thinking Archetypes

The systems thinking community has identified numerous *archetypes* that are seen over and over again in business, society, and the environment. Two of these models are explained below. Additional examples can be found online by searching for *systems thinking archetypes.*

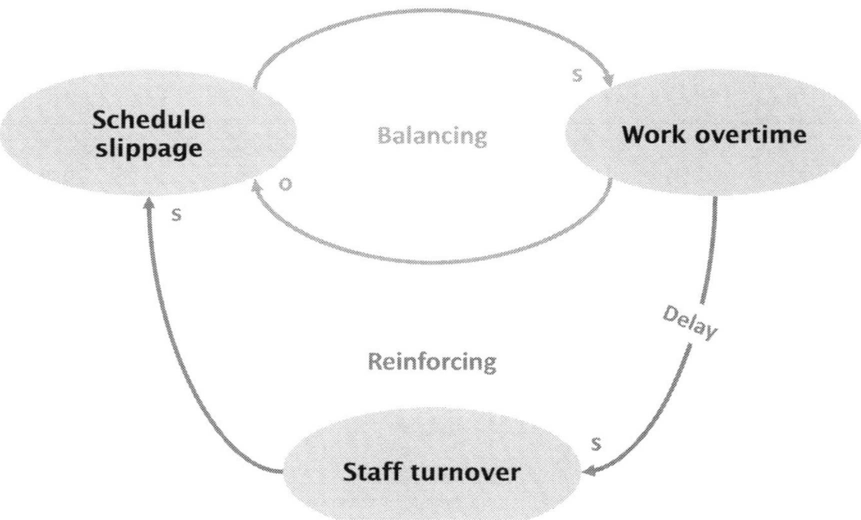

Figure 11-2: Causal Loop Diagram for Fixes that Fail

Fixes that fail. In this model, a problem (schedule slippage) is solved by a fix (working overtime) that has an immediate positive effect. In Figure 11-2 above, this is shown as a balancing loop: overtime reduces the schedule slippage and less slippage reduces the demand for overtime. However, if the schedule slippage continues (perhaps due to poor estimates), continued overtime is likely to lead staff turnover. Staff turnover is likely to cause further schedule slippage, and thus we have the reinforcing loop shown.

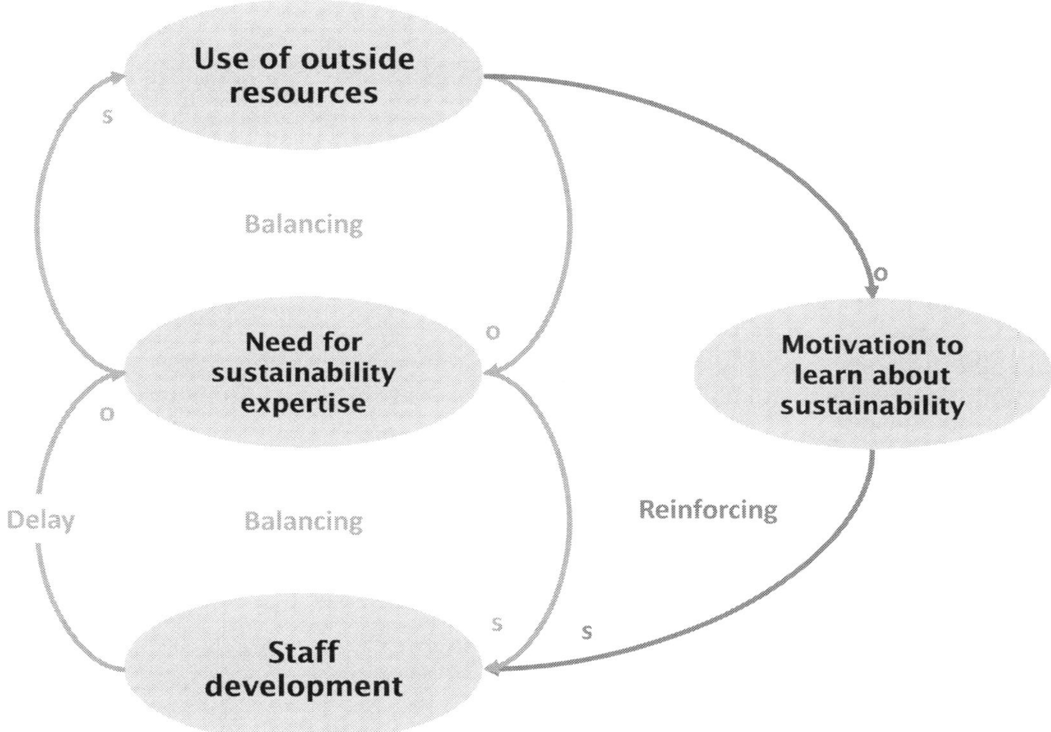

Figure 11-3: Causal Loop Diagram for Shifting the Burden

Shifting the burden. In this model, a project has a need for expertise in sustainability. The preferred solution is the lower balancing loop: develop the skills of the project team to provide the necessary expertise. However, staff development takes time, and there will be a delay before the desired expertise is available.

As a result, the project hires a consultant who can provide the expertise immediately as shown in the upper balancing loop. But the use of outside expertise is likely to lower the level of interest in staff development as shown in the reinforcing loop on the right. The decision to use outside help is a well-intentioned solution which seems to have solved the problem. But the underlying problem (lack of sustainability expertise) has not been addressed. As a result, the organization must continue to use outsiders.

11.3.2. The Sustainable Development Goals as a System

In Section 1.4, we presented the Sustainable Development Goals as seventeen independent items. In fact, all seventeen are connected and form a system where improvements in one area affect other areas. This is illustrated below in Figure 11-4 using the first three SDGs (the names of the variables have been modified slightly to make the relationships clearer).

Figure 11-4: Causal Loop Diagram of Selected SDGs

In the reinforcing loop on the right, reductions in poverty reduce hunger levels almost immediately, while less hunger has a delayed effect on poverty by making individuals better able to work. The relationship between poverty and good health is similar, but with delays in both effects: when poverty goes down, health levels go up, and when health levels improve, poverty goes down.

11.3.3. Waste Disposal

Systems thinking can also provide an overarching framework for understanding the industrial, governmental, and environmental interactions that play a role in sustainable development

For example, in the early days of the Industrial Era, the perception was that physical resources were unlimited and that Earth had an infinite capacity to absorb our wastes. Thus there was no reason to focus on reducing waste or reusing goods. With systems thinking, we recognize that earth is a closed system. We recognize that there is no "away" available to absorb our wastes — one person's "away" is someone else's backyard, water supply, or home.

11.3.4. Earth as a System

Our planet is a system that consists of the following subsystems:

- **Lithosphere** consists of the earth's core, mantle, crust, and soil.
- **Atmosphere** consists of the troposphere, stratosphere, mesosphere, thermosphere, and ionosphere.
- **Hydrosphere** consists of the solid, liquid, and gaseous water on earth, extending from the depths of the sea to the upper reaches of the troposphere.
- **Biosphere** is the collection of all earth's life forms, distributed in major life zones known as biomes — tundra, boreal forest, temperate deciduous forest, temperate grassland, desert, savannah, tropical rainforest, chaparral, freshwater, and marine.

As illustrated in Figure 11-5 below, there are ten possible interactions that can occur within this system. The double-headed arrows indicate that the cause-and-effect relationships go in both directions. For example, the arrow connecting the hydrosphere with the lithosphere refers to the effects of the lithosphere on the hydrosphere as well as the effects of the hydrosphere on the lithosphere.

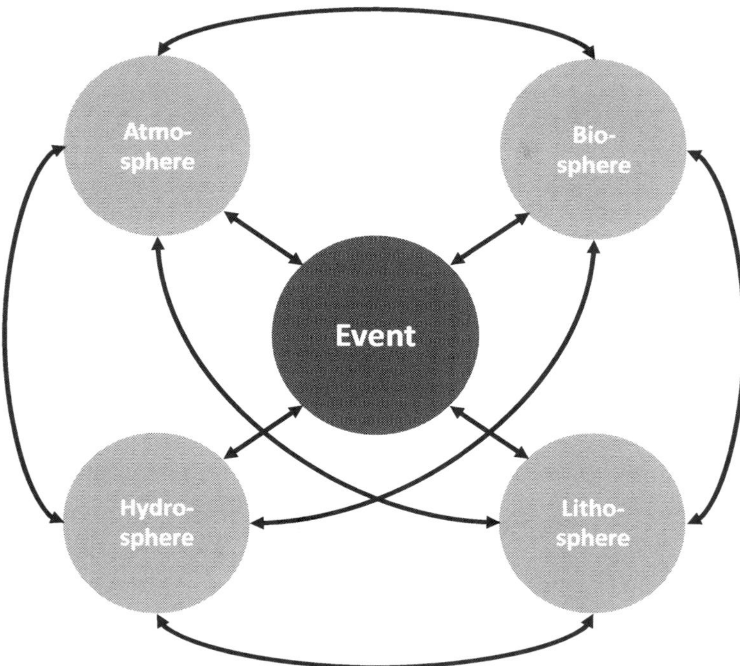

Figure 11-5: Interactions Between Spheres

By viewing this figure with a systems thinking perspective, we can see that an event can affect one or more of the spheres, and that the effect on each sphere can then affect the others. For example, a forest fire (event) may destroy all the plants in an area (event interacts with biosphere). The absence of plants could lead to an increase in erosion of soil (biosphere interacts with lithosphere). Increased amounts of soil entering streams can lead to increased turbidity, or muddiness, of the water (lithosphere interacts with hydrosphere). Increased turbidity of stream water can have negative impacts on the plants and animals that live in it (hydrosphere interacts with biosphere).

11.4. Summary

Systems thinking is a key aspect of sustainability and sustainable project management. While project management is often presented as a simple, linear, cause-and-effect process, the real world of project management often contains hidden relationships and interactions. By using systems thinking concepts, project managers are able to better understand the full extent of potential impacts that the project may cause and may also be able to better understand why seemingly beneficial interventions do not always result in positive outcomes.

PART FOUR: Standards

Notes

12. Standards Supporting Sustainable Projects

This chapter presents an overview of standards that support sustainability. Implementation of these standards by the performing organization can help facilitate the delivery of sustainable projects.

All of the standards in this chapter can be implemented by organizations in both the public and private sectors, irrespective of size, activity, or geographical location. GPM Global has incorporated many of the principles and concepts of these standards into PRiSM and P5.

12.1. International Organization for Standardization (ISO)

Most of the standards in this chapter were developed by the *International Organization for Standardization (ISO)*. ISO is an independent, non-governmental organization with a membership of over 160 national standards bodies. Through its members, ISO brings together experts to share knowledge and develop voluntary, consensus-based, market relevant standards that support innovation and provide solutions to global challenges.

ISO standards help to ensure that products and services are safe, reliable, and of good quality. They are open ended, multi-national, multi-cultural, and multi-linguistic. For many businesses, they are strategic tools that reduce costs by minimizing waste, reducing errors, and increasing productivity.

Organizational management systems based on these standards can help educate the project team about what the organization's sustainability priorities are. They can also provide support structures to understand where to focus.

12.2. Environmental Management Systems

An *environmental management system* is a structured system designed to help an organization manage the environmental impacts caused by its products, services, and activities. An EMS normally covers areas such as training, records management, inspections, objectives, and policies. For sustainable projects, the EMS of the performing organization can provide critical support for understanding how to ensure that the project approach and results are environmentally sound.

Subjects addressed by an EMS will typically include air pollution, water access, sewage and waste disposal, soil contamination, natural resource usage, and recycling-and-reuse practices.

An effective EMS can also help:

- Demonstrate compliance with statutory and regulatory requirements
- Increase engagement of employees
- Improve the organization's reputation (brand) and the confidence of stakeholders
- Achieve strategic business aims by addressing environmental issues

- Provide a competitive advantage through increased efficiency and reduced costs
- Encourage better environmental performance of suppliers by integrating them into the organization's systems

The ISO 14000 family provides a series of standards to help address environmental management. There are many standards in the family:

- Environmental management systems (8 standards)
- Environmental auditing and related environmental investigations (2 standards)
- Environmental labeling (6 standards)
- Environmental performance evaluation (5 standards)
- Lifecycle assessment (10 standards)
- Greenhouse gas management and related activities (13 standards)

ISO 14001:2015: Environmental management systems – Requirements with guidance for use is the base standard. It is applicable to any organization, regardless of size, type, and nature, and can be used in whole or in part to systematically improve environmental management.

12.3. Energy Management Systems

An *energy management system* (EnMS) helps an organization manage their energy use. Creating an EnMS involves developing and implementing an energy policy, setting targets for energy use, and designing action plans to reach them. This might include implementing energy-efficient technologies, reducing energy waste, or improving current processes to cut energy costs.

Energy management is increasing important because:

- Energy is critical to organizational operations and can be a major cost.
- In addition to the economic costs of energy, energy can impose environmental and societal costs by depleting resources and contributing to problems such as climate change.
- The development and deployment of technologies for new energy sources and renewable sources can take time.
- Individual organizations cannot control energy prices, government policies, or the global economy, but they can improve how they manage energy.

ISO 50001:2011 Energy management systems – Requirements with guidance for use provides a framework to enable organizations to:

- Develop a policy for more efficient use of energy
- Fix targets and objectives to meet the policy
- Use data to better understand and make decisions about energy use
- Measure the results
- Review how well the policy works
- Continually improve energy management

ISO 50001 is designed to help the organization get immediate benefits by making better use of its energy-consuming assets. There are also additional *indirect benefits*. Typical examples include:

- Improved control of operations leading to improved productivity
- Reduced noise
- Improved comfort levels in buildings
- Reduced maintenance costs
- Reduced downtime
- Reduced waste production
- Reduced water consumption
- Compliance with applicable legal requirements

12.4. Social Responsibility

Social responsibility (SR), also called corporate conscience, corporate citizenship, social performance, corporate social responsibility, or sustainable responsible business, is a form of corporate self-regulation. Social responsibility means that organizations actively comply with cultural values, ethical standards, the spirit of the law, and international norms. The intent of SR is to provide processes to accept, adopt, and integrate responsibility for the company's actions and to encourage it to have a positive impact on the environment and its employees, communities, consumers, and other stakeholders.

An organization's performance in relation to the society in which it operates and to its impact on the environment has become a critical part of measuring the organization's overall performance. The organization's level of Social Responsibility can influence:

- Competitive advantage
- Reputation
- Ability to attract and retain workers or members, customers, clients, or users
- Employee morale, commitment, and productivity
- View from investors, donors, sponsors, and the financial community
- Relationships with other companies, governments, media, and suppliers
- Peers, customers, and the community in which it operates

ISO 26000:2010 – Guidance on Social Responsibility is intended to assist organizations in contributing to sustainable development by being more socially responsible. It encourages them to go beyond legal compliance and seeks to promote a common understanding of social responsibility. When applying ISO 26000, organizations should consider societal, environmental, legal, cultural, political, and organizational diversity as well as differences in economic conditions, while being consistent with international norms of behavior.

ISO 26000 offers practical guidance to help an organization:

- Understand how it currently impacts society and contributes to sustainable development
- Identify, engage, and respect its stakeholder expectations
- Define which issues are relevant and significant and ensure they are prioritized for action
- Be in compliance with applicable laws and consistent with international norms of behavior
- Integrate responsible behavior throughout their organization and relationships

A related standard is *SA 8000:2014 Guidance Document for Social Accountability*. This standard is focused on managing human rights in the workplace. Implementing SA8000 can help:

- Achieve best practice in ethical employment, trading, and operations
- Engage and motivate employees
- Introduce greater transparency to the way the business is run
- Maintain existing business and attract new customers and investors
- Gain recognition as an socially accountable organization

12.5. Anti-bribery Management Systems

Anti-bribery management systems are intended to help organizations recognize and deal with the increasing level of threat from acts of bribery. *ISO 37001:2016 Anti-bribery management systems — Requirements with guidance for use* defines bribery as, "the offering, promising, giving, accepting or soliciting of an undue advantage of any value (which could be financial or non-financial), directly or indirectly, and irrespective of location(s), in violation of applicable law, as an inducement or reward for a person acting or refraining from acting in relation to the performance of that person's duties."

ISO 37001 supports establishing, implementing, maintaining, reviewing, and improving an anti-bribery management system. The standard deals with the following:

- Bribery in the public, private, and not-for-profit sectors
- Bribery by or of the organization
- Bribery by or of the organization's employees
- Bribery by or of the organization's business associates
- Direct and indirect bribery (e.g. a bribe offered or accepted through or by a third party)

The main benefit of an anti-bribery management system is, of course, that it can help to prevent bribery from occurring. It can also help to:

- Prevent losses from misappropriated funds.
- Avoid projects being undermined and not properly or safely carried out.
- Assisted in the organization's defense if it is prosecuted for bribery.

12.6. Sustainable Development in Communities

Sustainable development in communities refers to the potential for local communities (e.g., cities, towns, counties, and regional governments) to benefit themselves, society, and the environment by becoming more sustainable. *ISO 37101:2016 Sustainable development in communities – Management system for sustainable development – Requirements with guidance for use* is intended to support such efforts.

ISO 37101 provides guidance intended to:

- Improve the contribution of communities to sustainable development outcomes.
- Manage sustainability and foster smartness and resilience in communities, while taking into account the territorial boundaries to which it applies.

- Assess the performance of communities in progressing towards sustainable development.
- Fulfill compliance obligations.

12.7. Sustainable Procurement

Procurement is about how an organization manages its relationships with its direct and indirect suppliers. Procurement management, also called supply chain management, is a core competency for sustainable project management and is discussed in more detail in Section 6.7.

ISO 20400:2017 Sustainable procurement – Guidance provides an approach to help understand the risks and opportunities of *sustainable procurement*. It covers basics such as category management and the need for stakeholder input, as well as more advanced topics such as institutional complicity with unethical behavior and the need to deal with the entire supply chain and not just direct suppliers.

Implementing ISO 20400 can also serve to initiate discussions about sustainable procurement among customers and their supply chain.

The United Nations Office for Project Services (UNOPS) also offers guidance on sustainable procurement in its *Procurement Manual* (UNOPS, 2017). UNOPS has over 30 years of experience and is the provider of choice for many intergovernmental organizations, non-governmental organizations, international financial institutions, and foundations.

UNOPS makes sustainability an integral part of all its procurement practices by integrating its requirements with criteria that promote social progress, economic development, and the protection of the environment.

12.8. Quality Management Systems

The purpose of *quality management* is to help organizations provide products and services that meet all relevant customer needs and expectations and that comply with all relevant regulatory and statutory requirements. The ISO quality management standards require organizations to define their quality objectives and to continually improve their processes in order to reach them.

The ISO quality management standards are built on the following seven principles:

- Customer focus
- Leadership
- Engagement of people
- Process approach
- Improvement
- Evidence-based decision making
- Relationship management

Quality is achieved through a *quality management system*. A QMS is a set of interrelated or interacting elements that organizations use to formulate quality policies and quality objectives and to establish the processes needed to ensure that these policies are followed and these objectives are achieved. Although originally developed for manufacturing, QMSs today are typically applied to the entire organization.

Implementing a QMS will help an organization demonstrate to key stakeholders that it is capable of meeting customer requirements, enhancing customer satisfaction, and continually improving both its products and services. In turn, this can be expected to minimize risk, improve benefits, reduce costs, and enhance the organization's brand.

Standards in the ISO 9000 family include:

- *ISO 9000:2015: Quality management systems – Fundamentals and vocabulary* — covers basic concepts and language.
- *ISO 9001:2015: Quality management systems – Requirements* — sets out the requirements of a quality management system.
- *ISO 9004:2009: Quality management systems – Managing for the sustained success of an organization* — focuses on how to make a quality management system more efficient and effective.
- *ISO 10006:2017: Quality management – Guidelines to quality management in projects* — describes how to manage quality on a project.
- *ISO 19011:2011: Guidelines for auditing management systems* — sets out guidance on internal and external audits of quality management systems.

The relevance of quality management and quality management standards to projects is clearly stated in ISO 10006:2017:

> *There are two aspects to the application of quality management in projects; that of the project processes and that of the project's product. A failure to meet either of these dual aspects may have significant effects on the project's product, the project's customer and other interested parties, and the project organization.*
>
> *The creation and maintenance of process and product quality in a project requires a systematic approach. This approach should be aimed at ensuring that the stated and implied needs of the customer are understood and met, that other interested parties' needs are understood and evaluated, and that the originating organization's quality policy is taken into account for implementation in the management of the project.*

12.9. Asset Management Systems

An *asset management system* supports the process of developing, operating, maintaining, upgrading, and disposing of assets cost-effectively. An asset is an item, thing, or entity that has potential or actual value to an organization. Assets may be tangible (such as buildings or furniture) or intangible (such as human capital, intellectual property, or goodwill).

The outputs of a project will be assets for the performing organization.

The benefits of integrated, risk-based, whole lifecycle asset management include:

- Alignment of processes, resources, and functional contributions.
- Creating an audit trail for what is done, when, and why.

- Better understanding and usage of data to support informed and consistent decisions.
- Improved planning (especially of capital expenditures).
- Alignment and coordination of existing initiatives, including competency development.
- Greater engagement of the workforce.

ISO provides three standards to support asset management:

- *ISO 55000:2014 Asset management – Overview, principles and terminology* gives an overview of the subject and sets out its principles and terminology.
- *ISO 55001:2014 Asset management – Management systems – Requirements* specifies the requirements for the establishment, implementation, maintenance, and improvement of an asset management system.
- *ISO 55002:2014 Asset management – Management systems – Guidelines for the application of ISO 55001* provides advice and guidance for how to implement an asset management system that is in compliance with the requirements of ISO 55001.

AACE International also provides excellent guidance on asset management from a project perspective is its Total Cost Management (TCM) Framework and supporting guides. TCM supports sustainable projects as it manages cost throughout the lifecycle the asset.

TCM applies engineering practices, principles, and techniques to asset management. This includes various disciplines such as cost estimating, economic and financial analysis, cost engineering, planning and scheduling, cost and schedule performance measurement, and change control.

12.10. Risk and Opportunity Management

Risk and opportunity management covers how an organization deals with uncertain future events. It is a core competency for sustainable project management and is discussed in more detail in Section 5.4.

ISO 31000:2018, Risk management – Guidelines provides principles, a framework, and a process for managing risks and opportunities. There are numerous other standards on the subject including:

- Management of Risk (Axelos)
- Enterprise Risk Management (COSO)
- The Orange Book: Management of Risk — Principles and Concepts (HM Treasury)
- A Risk Management Standard (IRM)
- Governance, Risk, and Compliance (OCEG)
- Practice Standard for Project Risk Management (PMI)

12.11. Summary

This chapter has provided a summary of many relevant standards that apply to sustainability and sustainable project management. This chapter is not all encompassing, but rather highlights a range of relevant standards, summarizes the intent of those standards, and also highlights how and why each standard is relevant to sustainable project management.

Notes

13. Standards for Governance of Project Management

Numerous standards have emerged and been developed in the field of project management over the last ten years. These standards provide descriptions of good practice and are often an accumulation of expert knowledge that has been developed through consensus and codified into a written document.

Standards have been developed in the fields of:

- Governance
- Project Management
- Program Management
- Portfolio Management

Each of these topic will now be explored in more detail.

13.1. Governance Standards

A number of standards exist to provide guidance about appropriate systems of governance.

13.1.1. Governance of Project Management

Governance of Project Management (GoPM) was developed by the Association of Project Management (UK). Based on governance requirements and on the discipline of project management, the following 13 principles have been identified:

- The board has overall responsibility for governance of projects.
- The roles, responsibilities, and performance criteria for the governance of project management are clearly defined.
- Disciplined governance arrangements, supported by appropriate methods and controls, are applied throughout the project lifecycle.
- A coherent and supportive relationship is demonstrated between the overall business strategy and the project portfolio.
- All projects have an approved plan containing authorization points at which the business case is reviewed and approved. Decisions made at authorization points are recorded and communicated.
- The project business case is supported by relevant and realistic information that provides a reliable basis for making authorization decisions.
- The board or its delegated agents decide when independent scrutiny of projects and project management systems is required, and implement such scrutiny accordingly.
- There are clearly defined criteria for reporting project status and for the escalation of risks and issues to the levels required by the organization.

- The organization fosters a culture of improvement and of frank internal disclosure of project information.
- Project stakeholders are engaged at a level that is commensurate with their importance to the organization and in a manner that fosters trust.

Applying these principles would help avoid common causes of project failure, including:

- A lack of a clear link with key strategic priorities.
- A lack of clear senior management and, in government projects, ministerial ownership and leadership.
- A lack of effective engagement with stakeholders.
- A lack of skills and proven approach to project and risk management.
- A lack of understanding of, or contact with, supply industry at senior levels.
- Evaluation of projects by initial price rather than by long-term value for money.
- Too little attention to breaking down development and implementation into manageable steps.

13.1.2. AS/NZS 8016: 2013 Governance of IT enabled projects

While this standard was developed for governance of IT projects, its principles apply equally to non-IT projects. The standard articulates six principles for project governance:

- **Responsibility** — the responsibility for realization of value from projects involving investment in IT is defined with understood and accepted roles for the governance and management of projects including realization of benefits.
- **Strategy** — the organization's strategy maximizes the potential for success from projects involving investment in IT.
- **Investment** — investments in projects are made for valid reasons, on the basis of appropriate and ongoing analysis, and with clear and transparent decision-making. This includes ensuring that the benefits to be obtained, the full scope of activities required to achieve the benefits, and the mechanisms for measuring the benefits are clearly understood.
- **Performance** — each project is managed to achieve the agreed outcomes while managing risks to the organization.
- **Conformance** — each project conforms to external regulations and internal policies.
- **Human Behavior** — each project demonstrates a respect for human behavior in the planning and management of activities and in the resultant deliverables and their use in the changes to business processes.

13.2. Project Management Standards

13.2.1. PRojects IN Controlled Environments (PRINCE2)

Governance in PRINCE 2 is encapsulated through the project board and its role in directing the project. This specifically involves:

- Authorizing project initiation
- Authorizing a project business case and project plan

- Authorizing a stage or exception plan
- Providing project management direction and control
- Confirming project closure

13.2.2. A Guide to the Project Management Body of Knowledge

The so-called *PMBOK Guide* takes a largely process-oriented view of individual projects. To ensure appropriate project governance, the PMBOK Guide suggests that the following be designed and built into the project:

- Project success and deliverable acceptance criteria
- Process to identify, escalate, and resolve issues
- Defined roles and relationships
- Processes for communication of information
- Project decision-making processes
- Guidelines for aligning governance and strategy
- Project lifecycle approach
- Process for project stage/phase reviews
- Process for scope/schedule/budget reviews

13.2.3. ISO 21500:2012 Guidance on project management

The ISO 21500 standard was produced under the guidance of the ISO Technical Committee 258, a group of over 60 representatives from project management and standards bodies around the world. ISO 21500 suggests that project governance includes the following:

- Defining the management structure
- The policies, processes, and methodologies to be used
- Limits of authority for decision-making
- Stakeholder responsibilities and accountabilities
- Interactions such as reporting and the escalation of issues or risks

ISO 21500 also identifies that the responsibility for maintaining the appropriate governance of a project is usually assigned either to the project sponsor or to a project steering committee.

13.2.4. Portfolio, Programme, and Project Maturity Model (Projects)

Maturity models such as P3M3 can provide a useful lens through which to examine an organization's project management governance practices. When examining the project level using P3M3, one would expect to see:

- Common definition of project boards (or their equivalent) and their key roles and responsibilities.
- Project boards in place on most projects unless there is a clear reason for them not to be.
- Central body that monitors and influences progress of all projects and the optimal balance of current projects.

- Consolidated progress reporting on all projects.
- All key roles and responsibilities documented with individual terms of reference.
- Project ideas evaluated against consistent criteria prior to approval.
- Centralized decision-making to ensure that projects fit the organization's ongoing needs.
- Functional activities of project sponsor or project executive can be demonstrated for all projects.
- Evidence of project sponsor or project executives ensuring that projects maintain alignment with organizational strategy, with interventions as appropriate.
- Auditable decisions.
- Clear reporting lines set and maintained.
- Legislative and regulatory requirements built into guidelines.
- Evidence of structured start-up and closure of projects under clear business control.

13.3. Program Management Standards

13.3.1. Managing Successful Programs

The *Managing Successful Programmes* (MSP) standard identifies governance as a key theme for program management and suggests that governance at the program level is a key control framework through which programs deliver their change objectives while maintaining corporate visibility and control. MSP suggests that the need for governance over change is manifested in two ways:

- Control and ownership of the change program
- The control and stewardship of the organization as a corporate entity

It also identifies a number of governance themes:

- Organization
- Vision
- Leadership and stakeholder engagement
- Benefits realization management
- Blueprint design and delivery
- Planning and control
- Business case
- Risk and issue management
- Quality management

13.3.2. The Standard for Program Management

PMI's standard for program management identifies a number of key governance-related actions for the program manager including:

- Establishing agreements for the sponsoring organization's oversight and resource commitments.

- Maintaining program goal alignment with the strategic vision.
- Endorsing and enabling program components (projects).
- Communicating program risks and uncertainties.
- Communicating and addressing program issues.
- Conducting periodic program reviews.
- Establishing, assessing, and enforcing conformance with organizational standards.
- Facilitating engagement with program stakeholders and establishing clear expectations.

The PMI standard also highlights program board responsibilities:

- Program governance and envisioning
- Program approval, endorsement, and initiation
- Ensuring appropriate program funding
- Establishing a program governance plan
- Identifying program success criteria
- Approving program approach and plans
- Supporting the program
- Overseeing program compliance and reporting
- Overseeing program quality standards and planning
- Monitoring program progress and assessing the need for change
- Reviewing the program at key decision points
- Approving component (project) initiation of transition
- Approving the recommendation to close the program

13.3.3. Portfolio, Programme, and Project Maturity Model (Programs)

Maturity models such as P3M3 can provide a useful lens through which to examine an organization's program management governance practices. When examining the program level using P3M3, one would expect to see:

- Legal and regulatory controls are embedded in the program lifecycle and processes.
- Decision-making within the program has audit trails.
- Process exists for stopping or changing a program's direction.
- Clear reporting lines within the program, including to senior management.
- Personal objectives and program management responsibilities defined for key individuals.
- Standard program organizational structure available for use by each program and deployed flexibly.
- Reporting structure in place, used consistently to keep the business informed of program progress, and interweaving with current business performance reporting.
- Difference between responsibility and accountability clearly developed within program management framework.
- Responsibility for program processes clearly defined and linked to organizational responsibilities where appropriate.

- Central gathering of business performance information as well as program performance information.
- Business change managers or leaders embedded within program organization and fundamental to decision-making with adequate authority to orchestrate any changes required.
- Business lifecycle activities (e.g., year-end) factored into change plans.

13.4. Portfolio Management Standards

13.4.1. *Management of Portfolios*

The *Management of Portfolios* (MoP) standard has a strong focus on governance alignment to ensure consistency with the wider organizational governance approach. In doing so, it calls for:

- A shared vision for the portfolio
- Clearly defined roles, responsibilities, and accountabilities
- Consistency with organizational governance practices and structures
- Shared understanding
- An agreed escalation process
- Aligned meeting schedules
- Sub-portfolios periodically reviewed by the organizational portfolio governance body
- Regular reviews of business cases and progress
- Support by a portfolio office that establishes, operates, and develops the portfolio management process

13.4.2. *The Standard for Portfolio Management*

This PMI standard is primarily a process-based standard in which a portfolio is managed through a formal and explicit process. The standard mixes aspects of portfolio management functions and portfolio governance. This standard identifies a number of key functions:

- Developing the portfolio management plan
- Defining the portfolio
- Optimizing the portfolio
- Authorizing the portfolio
- Providing portfolio oversight

A key aspect of this standard is identification of the need for a:

- Governance model (i.e., a portfolio management framework)
- Portfolio office to provide guidance and oversight

13.4.3. Portfolio, Programme, and Project Maturity Model (Portfolios)

Maturity models such as P3M3 can provide a useful lens through which to examine an organization's project management governance practices. When examining the portfolio level using P3M3, one would expect to see:

- Established and documented policies, standards, processes, and governance for change investments, and an executive board-owned structure to oversee portfolio performance.
- Clear, defined vision for organizational change with senior management demonstrating commitment to it.
- Well-defined portfolio aligned with strategic objectives and priorities.
- Clear governance structure ensuring that all initiatives are evaluated, prioritized, and approved based on strategic objectives, and business cases are continually reviewed for validity and viability.
- An organization portfolio office that monitors effectiveness of governance and level of stakeholder engagement for all initiatives.
- Legislative and regulatory requirements incorporated into portfolio management decision and controls processes.
- Governance controls integrated into portfolio controls.
- Business performance information acquired and reviewed by organization portfolio office.
- Process ownership and related decision-making responsibilities are clearly defined.

13.5. Summary

This chapter has provided a description of the key governance elements as described in key project, program, and portfolio standards. This chapter is not intended to be all encompassing, but rather highlights the manner in which various standards describe the governance functions, and should be read in conjunction with Chapter 7.

Notes

Authors

Joel Carboni	Dr. Joel Carboni has over 23 years' experience in project, program, and portfolio management for Fortune 500 companies and regional government. He is a graduate of Ball State University and holds a Ph.D. in Sustainable Development and Environment. His body of work includes contributions to international standards for project management and advocacy for adoption of the UN Sustainable Development Goals by the project management profession. Joel is an Eagle Scout, the recipient of the 2013 IPMA Achievement Award for applying sustainable principles to project delivery, and was granted the honor of knighthood in the Order of St. George. He believes that sustainable projects are the key to regenerating our planet and ensuring that future generations can thrive. A regular speaker at universities, conferences, and summits, he has traveled the world planting seeds for social, environmental, and economic stewardship.
William R. Duncan	William R. Duncan has over 40 years of management and consulting experience including five years with a major international consulting firm. He is a graduate of Brown University in Providence, RI and has done post-graduate work in computer science at Boston University. He was the primary author of the original (1996) version of *A Guide to the Project Management Body of Knowledge (PMBoK Guide),* the most widely used project management guide in the world. In addition, his "process model" of project management was used to organize both *ISO 10006, Guidance on quality in project management* and *ISO 21500, Guidance on project management.* He has authored over 40 articles for publications such as the *Project Management Journal*, *PMNetwork*, *Projects@Work*, and *Chief Projects Officer.* He has presented papers at conferences sponsored by IPMA-USA, PMI, AIPM, FOSTAS, and others. He is currently Director of Certification for both GPM Global and IPMA-USA.
Mónica González	Mónica González is Industrial Engineer, has over 27 years' experience in Electric Power Companies, public and private, with a specialization for two years in Houston (Texas, USA) in automation of electrical grids. She has a MBA (Catholic University of Cordoba, Argentina), a MPM (ADEN and Stetson University, USA), and Certifications PMP® (PMI), and GPM-m® (GPM Global). In the past 18 years, she has involved with Organizational Integrated Management Systems according to the International Standards. Active actor of the ISO Standards, she was contributor member of the ISO PC/TC for Project, Program and Portfolio Management. Member of the GPM Global Leadership Executive Team and main contributor to the PRiSM Methodology. As a strong advocate of the UNGC, her mission is to contribute to Global Sustainability, an imperative of the Society as a whole, tending to improve the quality of life, well-being and safety of people, rational use of resources and energy efficiency. Her Legacy is Project Management for Peace.

Peter Milsom	Peter Milsom is a Certified Management Consultant and a Fellow of the Canadian Association of Management Consultants as well as an advocate for sustainable development. He holds over fifty professional certifications and designations and is a career entrepreneur. He is an active and passionate volunteer committing substantial time to the development of the project management profession through associations, standards development, and the United Nations. He has represented Canada as a subject matter expert for a number of ISO standards and serves as the convener for the *ISO 21500 Guidance on project management* refresh. He has also worked actively on standards development for GPM, IPMA, APMG, GAPPS, AXELOS, and PMI. Peter is an accomplished speaker and author and has worked in over fifty countries. He advocates for sensible, sustainable change delivery practice, as well as adoption and delivery of the UN's Sustainable Development Goals.
Michael Young	Michael Young is a serial entrepreneur with a passion for project management. He has over 20 years' experience working in project, program, and portfolio management across many sectors including government, defense, engineering IT, and logistics. Michael's voluntary contribution to project management is remarkable, having developed numerous ISO standards 258, as one of the authors of IPMA's ICB4, as a member of the IPMA research board, and through over 18 years' service in various roles with the Australian Institute of Project Management. Michael's work has been featured in BRW, the *Australian Financial Review*, and *SmartCompany*. He has received over 25 awards, including Australian Business Award's for project management, innovation, and sustainability. He also managed the Australian IT Project of the Year in 2006. As a prolific author and speaker, Michael actively advocates for an evolution of project management and the delivery of sustainable change.

References

Aguirre, DeAnne, and Alpern, Micah. "10 Principles of Leading Change Management." Retrieved March 6, 2018. https://www.strategy-business.com/article/00255?gko=9d35b

Association of Change Management Professionals. *Standard for Change Management*. Winter Spring, Florida USA: The Association of Change Management Professionals, 2014

Bekker, M.H., and Steyn, H. "Project governance: Definition and Framework." *Journal of Contemporary Management*. Volume 6, Issue 1, Jan 2009, p. 214–228.

Caravel Group. "A Review of Project Governance Effectiveness in Australia." Retrieved March 6, 2018. http://infrastructureaustralia.gov.au/policy-publications/publications/files/CARAVEL_GROUP_Project_Governance_Effectiveness_March_2013.pdf

Dodgson, Mark and Gann, David. *Innovation: A very short introduction*. Oxford: Oxford University Press, 2010

Ferrell, O.C., et al. *Business Ethics: Ethical Decision Making & Cases*. Boston: Cencage Learning, 2017

Fuller, Sieglinde. "Life-Cycle Cost Analysis (LCCA)." Retrieved March 6, 2018. https://www.wbdg.org/resources/life-cycle-cost-analysis-lcca

International Organization for Standardization. *ISO 21500:2012 - Guidance on project management*. Geneva, Switzerland: ISO, 2012

Jenner, Steve. *Managing Benefits*. Norwich, UK: The Stationery Office, 2014

Kahneman, Daniel. *Thinking, Fast and Slow*. New York: Farrar, Strauss and Giroux, 2011

Kerry, James, et al. "Two-thirds of Great Barrier Reef hit by back-to-back mass coral bleaching." Retrieved March 6, 2018. https://www.jcu.edu.au/news/releases/2017/april/two-thirds-of-great-barrier-reef-hit-by-back-to-back-mass-coral-bleaching

Kim, W. Chan, and Mauborgne, Renée. Blue Ocean Strategy: How to Create Uncontested Market Space and Make the Competition Irrelevant. Cambridge, MA: HBS Press, 2003

National Academy of Science. "Proceedings." Retrieved March 6, 2018. http://www.pnas.org

Office of Government Commerce. Management of Value. Norwich, UK: The Stationery Office, 2010

Senge, Peter M. *The Fifth Discipline: The Art and Practice of the Learning Organization*. New York: Doubleday, 1990

Transparency International. "Corruption Perceptions Index." Retrieved March 6, 2018. https://www.transparency.org

United Nations Global Compact. *IMPACT: Transforming Business, Changing the World*. Retrieved March 6, 2018. https://www.unglobalcompact.org/library/1331

United Nations. "Sustainable Development Goals." Retrieved March 6, 2018. http://www.un.org/sustainabledevelopment/

Waters Foundation. "Habits of a Systems Thinker." Retrieved March 6, 2018. http://watersfoundation.org/systems-thinking/habits-of-a-systems-thinker/

Notes

Notes

Made in the USA
Las Vegas, NV
06 March 2024